PRESENTED BY

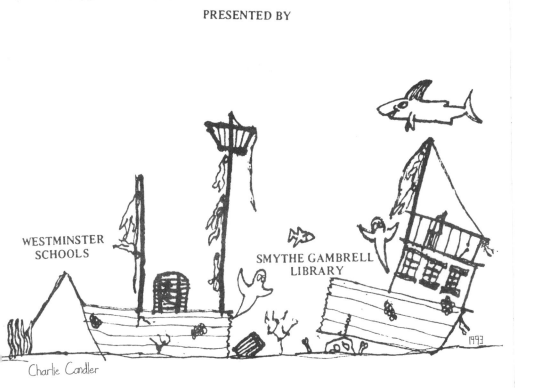

WESTMINSTER
SCHOOLS

SMYTHE GAMBRELL
LIBRARY

Charlie Candler

1993

THE PHILIPPINES
PACIFIC CROSSROADS

DISCOVERING *our* **HERITAGE**

by Margaret Sullivan

DILLON PRESS
New York

Maxwell Macmillan Canada
Toronto
Maxwell Macmillan International
New York Oxford Singapore Sydney

Photo Credits

All photos courtesy of Mark Downey except for the image of the neolithic pot on page 25, taken by Julius Garcia.

The author wishes to thank San Carlos University, Cebu, for its kind permission to photograph its replica of the neolithic pot discovered in the Mununggal Cave in Palawan.

Library of Congress Cataloging-in-Publication Data

Sullivan, Margaret W.
    The Philippines : Pacific crossroads / by Margaret Sullivan.
      p. cm. — (Discovering our heritage)
    Includes bibliographical references and index.
    Summary: Describes the geography, history, folklore, family life, and culture of the Philippines, as well as those inhabitants who have immigrated to the United States.
    ISBN 0-87518-548-7
    1. Philippines—Juvenile literature. [1. Philippines.] I Title. II. Series.
DS655.S85   1993
959.9—dc20   92-37093

Dillon Press
Macmillan Publishing Company
866 Third Avenue
New York, NY 10022

Maxwell Macmillan Canada, Inc.
1200 Eglinton Avenue East
Suite 200
Don Mills, Ontario M3C 3N1

Macmillan Publishing Company is part of the Maxwell Communication Group of Companies.

First edition

10 9 8 7 6 5 4 3 2 1

For Sam, Rebecca, and Grace,
my grandchildren whose parents were children in the Philippines,
and Miguel, Mirella, Andy, Martin, Cecilia, and Marianne,
my Borromeao-clan godchildren

Acknowledgments
This book was made possible because so many generous friends over the years have helped me grow in my understanding of the Philippines, patiently answered my questions, and assisted Mark Downey when he traveled there to take photographs. We are both grateful to them all, particularly: Ching Calub, Malcolm Churchill, Jun de los Reyes, PCVC; Evelyn and John Forbes, Honeybee Hubahib, Jaime Picornell, Marisol Putong, Peachy Villanueva, and Jim and Joan Wilson.

Dr. Bernadita Reyes Churchill, Professor of History at the University of the Philippines, read the manuscript and gave me much useful guidance.

Pam Benson's 1991-1992 sixth graders at Sidwell Friends School in Washington, D.C. made helpful comments. So did my grown children, Asianists Jerry and Charley Sullivan, and teacher Gay Abrams.

My editor, Joyce Stanton, of Dillon Press deserves special credit. Above all, my husband, Dan Sullivan, whose work brought us to the Philippines in the first place, provided continuing encouragement and sound advice.

Contents

Fast Facts about the Philippines

Official Name: Republic of the Philippines

Capital: Manila

Location: The Philippines is an island nation off the southeastern coast of the Asian mainland. It consists of more than 7,000 islands lying in a chain between the South China Sea on the west and the Pacific Ocean on the east. To the north its neighbor is Taiwan. To the south lie Indonesia and Malaysia.

Area: 115,831 square miles. *Greatest distances*: east-west, 688 miles; north-south, 1,152 miles. *Coastline:* 14,400 miles.

Elevation: *Highest:* Mount Apo, on the island of Mindanao, 9,692 feet above sea level. *Lowest:* sea level along the coast. The Mindanao Deep (also called the Philippine Trench) to the east of Mindanao is one of the deepest chasms in the ocean floor, 34,440 feet below sea level.

Climate: Tropical, in the typhoon belt.

Population: 66.6 million (1990 estimate) *Distribution:* about 55 percent rural, 45 percent urban. Nearly 95 percent of all Filipinos live on the chain's 11 largest islands.

Form of Government: A republic headed by a president. The constitutional government is modeled after that of the United States with a legislative branch, consisting of a Senate and a House of Representatives, and an independent judiciary.

Important Products: *Natural Resources:* timber, gold, copper, nickel, iron, cobalt, silver, and petroleum. *Agriculture:* sugar, coconut products, rice, corn, pineapples, and bananas. *Industries:* textiles, pharmaceuticals, chemicals, wood products, food processing, electronics assembly.

Basic Unit of Money: Peso

Languages: Pilipino (based on Tagalog, one of the major languages) is the official national language. English is the language of the government and most schools and universities.

Religion: Some 92 percent of all Filipinos are Christian: 83 percent of the population is Catholic and 9 percent Protestant. About 5 percent are Muslim. The remaining population practice traditional religions.

Flag: A field of two horizontal bands, blue on top, red on the bottom, joined at the staff side with a white triangle. Centered on the triangle is a yellow, eight-rayed sun that represents liberty. The rays stand for the eight provinces around Manila that revolted in 1896, starting the Philippine War for Independence. In each corner of the triangle is a yellow star, representing the three major divisions of the country: Luzon, the Visayas, and Mindanao.

National Anthem: *Bayang Magiliw* (Beloved Country)

Major Holidays: Independence Day (June 12), Christmas, New Year's Day, Good Friday, Easter, All Saints' Day (November 1), *Hari Raya* (following Ramadan, the ninth month of the Muslim year), and *Hari Raya Haji* (marking the *haji*; the pilgrimage that Muslims try to make once in a lifetime to the holy city of Mecca).

1. A Nation of Islands

The Republic of the Philippines is a nation of islands—more than 7,000 of them, scattered over a half million square miles of tropical sea.

A few of the islands are large. Flying the length of Mindanao, the Philippines' second-biggest island, for instance, takes almost as long as flying from San Francisco to Los Angeles. You pass Mount Apo, the country's highest volcano, where conservationists are trying to save the monkey-eating eagle from extinction. You also see jungle-covered mountains, farmland, cities, towns, and villages, just as you do on all the bigger islands.

Luzon, the largest island, has miles of low-lying, fertile plains ideal for growing rice and sugarcane. It also has the Gran Cordillera, rugged mountains so high they are frequently lost in the clouds. Centuries ago, the mountain people living there constructed one of the wonders of the world: spectacular pond-terraces for raising rice, connected by a complex network of irrigation ditches. These terraces contour the slopes and valleys of over 100 square miles of the Gran Cordillera. The builders' descendants still maintain and use them today.

From the air, many other Philippine islands look like

tiny green specks surrounded by water so shallow and clear that the sandy yellow sea bottom shows through it. Beyond them, the sea shimmers bright azure and then inky blue as it gets deeper. The Mindanao Deep, one of the deepest ocean trenches in the world, runs along the east coast of Mindanao. Its bottom is about seven miles below the ocean's surface.

The Philippines is part of Southeast Asia. The islands—separated by narrow ocean passages called straits—stretch more than a thousand miles from north to south. To the south lie Indonesia and Malaysia. To the north is Taiwan. Vietnam and China are some 600 miles to the west and northwest across the South China Sea. The Pacific Ocean forms a vast border to the east.

How Many Islands?

High tide or low? It makes a difference in how many islands there are in the Philippines. At high tide, the flattest coral islands disappear below the ocean surface. No one, therefore, is exactly sure of the total. The official count is 7,107. If you could group all of them into one big island, it would be about the same size as Arizona or Italy.

Only 2,773 of the islands are even big enough to have been given names. People live on about 1,000 of them. But 94 percent of the 66.6 million Filipinos are crammed onto just 11 islands. Between Luzon and Mindanao are a

Rice terraces in the Gran Cordillera—an extraordinary engineering feat accomplished centuries ago

belt of islands called the Visayas. These islands—Bohol, Cebu, Leyte, Masbate, Negros, Panay, and Samar—are also referred to as the central Philippines. South of the main part of Luzon is Mindoro. Beyond that, like a bony finger pointing at Malaysia, is Palawan.

Another island group, known as the Sulu Archipelago, extends from Mindanao southwest toward Indonesia. An archipelago is a group or chain of islands. The Philippines is actually a large archipelago and Sulu is a smaller one within it.

Because the larger islands have mountainous interiors, most Filipinos live on the coastal lowlands, which are often narrow. Each year, the Philippines is getting more and more crowded. Its population is among the fastest-growing in the world. Although the amount of land suitable for living on has stayed about the same, for every one Filipino in 1948, there were three in 1991.

Several of the larger islands are still at least partly covered with tropical rain forests. But deforestation is a problem. The forests are being logged for lumber and cleared for farmland. The rounded mountains of Cebu, however, have been scrubby and barren for years. Its forests were cut by the Spanish colonizers and shipped to Mexico in the 17th and 18th centuries.

Ring of Fire

The Philippines is part of the Ring of Fire, the chain of volcanoes that circles the Pacific Ocean. The country has 21 active and over 200 inactive, or dormant, volcanoes. Mount Mayon, in southern Luzon, is a perfect volcanic cone that is often shown on tourist posters.

In June and July of 1991, Mount Pinatubo in central Luzon erupted. It had been dormant for over 600 years. Ash fell like heavy snow as far as 50 miles away, crumpling roofs of buildings. When heavy rains followed, enormous mudflows engulfed towns and covered acres of some of the best rice land. Many people were killed. Thousands more were forced to flee, losing everything. A year later, Pinatubo was still erupting occasionally.

Also because the islands lie along the Ring of Fire, they experience many earthquakes. Some, like one in Luzon in 1990, do enormous damage, demolishing buildings, killing people, and leaving many homeless. Most just shake the house, rattle the dishes, and tilt the pictures on the walls.

The Philippines is also in the typhoon belt. Typhoons are storms with destructive winds and torrential rains that sweep out of the Pacific Ocean. Between July and October each year, as many as 15 typhoons hit the Philippines, and five or six of them do great damage.

A Tropical Climate

The Philippine islands lie just north of the equator, in the part of the world known as the tropics. The sun rises about six o'clock every morning and sets about six at night, with only a small change throughout the year. The lowlands are hot, above 80°F, and humid year-round. But in the mountains, it gets quite chilly, particularly at night.

The biggest seasonal change is between wet and dry. In much of the country, the wet, or monsoon, season is from June to November. During those months, prevailing winds off the Pacific bring extremely hard rains almost daily. These can cause flooding. Starting in December or January skies are usually clear and there is little or no rain. By April or May it is often extremely hot. Everyone is anxious for the rains to come again. Only Mindanao has even rainfall throughout the year.

One Nation, Many Heritages

The Philippines is a crossroads in the Pacific. Down through time, settlers have come to the islands from near and far, making the country a unique blend of peoples and cultures. Because the islands are in Southeast Asia, all Filipinos can be considered Asians. Most of them belong to the broad group of Austronesian peoples, who live throughout the islands of Southeast Asia and much of the South Pacific (which also includes Hawaiian islanders). Their languages are related and their cultures are similar. These people have been living in the Philippine islands for 5,000 years or more. A very few Filipinos are Negritos, who are probably the descendants of even earlier inhabitants of the islands.

A significant community of Filipinos are of Chinese ancestry. Even more Filipinos are part Chinese. Filipinos call people of mixed islander and other ancestry "mestizos." Some Filipino mestizos are part Spanish or American.

More than 400 years ago, Spanish colonizers came

to the islands. They ruled for over 300 years. Their culture has played an important role in shaping life in the Philippines. Americans governed the islands for some 50 years after the Spanish. The Philippines, combining many heritages into one, became an independent country in 1946.

Geography has also contributed to the diversity of the nation. Today, some 87 languages are spoken in the Philippines. Historically, the steep mountain spines of the islands have acted as barriers, isolating and dividing people. The sea, meanwhile, has been like a highway, linking communities by boat.

This has helped determine where different languages are spoken. Everyone on the island of Cebu speaks Cebuano, for example. So do the people across the strait on the next island west, Negros. Beyond the mountains of central Negros, however, people speak a different language, Ilongo.

City, Village, Farm, and Forest Dwellers

Present-day Filipinos live in modern cities, quiet towns, and simple barrios (small villages). Some live in fishing communities built on stilts over the sea, and a few live deep in the rain forests. More than half of all the people— men, women, and children—are farmers. Some own their small farms. Many others work on haciendas (plantations)

In the countryside many Filipinos live in houses built on stilts, like this one.

belonging to well-to-do landlords. Although some Filipinos are extremely wealthy, two in every three are desperately poor.

Nearly ten million people live in Manila, the Philippine's capital and largest city, located on Luzon. More are moving to Manila every day because they think they can make a better living there. It is a sprawling city of sharp contrasts. Parts of Manila look like suburban sections of San Diego or Miami, with pleasant houses and gardens. Other areas are jammed with hastily built shacks. The business district, Makati, is filled with skyscrapers. People with enough money can watch television, buy food in supermarkets, eat Big Macs, and work with computers. Others struggle to barely make a living.

The Philippines has other cities as well. Like Manila, the port city of Cebu, on the island of Cebu in the Visayas, is a transportation hub. Davao, in southeastern Mindanao, is the country's second-largest city. It has over 600,000 residents. Zamboanga, on the western tip of Mindanao, is an old trading center known for its flowers. Bacolod, on the western coast of Negros, is in the heart of the sugar-

Cebu City at night

growing area. Iloilo is a port and regional trading center on Panay.

While the cities are overflowing with people, only 24 individuals make up the entire Tasaday tribe. Up until 20 years ago, the Tasaday were isolated deep in the Mindanao jungle. They lived in caves, used simple stone tools they made themselves, and searched the forest daily for food. Sometime in the early 1960s one of them encountered a less isolated group of people also living in the rain forest. As those people told others, news that the Tasaday existed reached the outside world. In 1971 officials from Manila visited them and their cave. The government has since set aside a protected area of land for them on Mindanao.

Coconuts, Crafts, and Components

Filipinos earn their livings in many different ways. Some are engaged in traditional occupations like agriculture, fishing, or crafts. Others are involved in a variety of industries.

Agriculture is a major part of the Philippine economy. Farmers raise much of their own food plus crops to sell within the country and abroad. They grow rice, corn, vegetables, and an enormous variety of tropical fruits. Many of the pineapples and bananas are exported to other countries. Sugarcane and coconuts, the other important agricultural products, are processed before they are shipped outside the country.

The Philippines is one of the world's biggest producers of sugar. Sugarcane is usually raised on haciendas. Cutting it in the sunbaked fields is exhausting work. After the cane is cut, it is taken to a factory where the sweet juice is squeezed from it. The juice is cooked into molasses syrup and processed into sugar. The leftover cane pulp, bagasse, is sometimes made into paper.

The country is also a major producer of coconuts. Most are turned into copra, the dried meat of the coconut. Coconut meat is mainly solidified oil. On smaller farms, farmers crack the nuts themselves, take off the shell, and dry the meat in the sun. However, most copra is processed in factories in the towns. In either case, the copra is then pressed so the last bit of oil comes out. Coconut oil is valuable. It is used for cooking or sent to places like the United States, where it is used to make products like candy, soap, and candles.

Philippine waters are rich in seafood. It is no surprise then that fishing is important. Some fishermen go out in little boats and catch mainly small fish like anchovies and sardines to eat themselves and to sell locally. Others build fishtraps in the shallow seas and catch bigger seafood like mackerel, flounder, and squid. Larger boats that can go out to deeper waters catch fish like grouper and red snapper, which are shipped to towns and cities. They process the tuna and other big fish they catch on board.

Fields of rice—the Philippines most important crop—stretch far into the distance.

Huge fishing ships come into Philippine waters from other countries.

While much fishing is done with nets, sometimes fishermen throw dynamite and then gather the stunned fish that float to the surface. This damages all the fish and destroys the coral reefs as well. Dynamite fishing is illegal but hard to stop.

Recently, aquaculture has become an important industry. In areas of shallow seawater, fish-farmers build enclosed ponds for raising fish, shrimp, or crabs, which they harvest regularly.

The Philippines has developed many of its natural

resources. Timber is the most important. Both logs and sawed lumber are exported. Mining is important, too. Philippine deposits of chromite, copper, and nickel are among the largest in the world. Gold, silver, and cobalt are also leading mineral products.

Filipinos are famous for their handicrafts. They make baskets of all kinds. Originally, these were for local, everyday use. Now they are made for export. Many baskets found in stores in the United States come from the Philippines.

Because there are so many seashells around them, Filipinos have learned to fashion them into everything from windowpanes and lamp shades to plates and jewelry. They also make beautiful woven and embroidered products and wood carvings. The country is known, too, for its rattan furniture, which is mostly sold abroad. Rattan is a tough jungle vine, and Filipinos are now trying to grow it on farms.

The Philippines has many modern factories, located mainly around Manila. Clothes and electronics, including computer components, are the major exports. Filipinos also process pharmaceuticals (drugs, like aspirin and antibiotics) and chemicals.

People are a particularly big source of money for the country. Foreign tourists visit the Philippines to enjoy its tropical climate, splendid beaches, beautiful scenery, and friendly people. They spend money and buy things. Many

Filipinos, on the other hand, cannot find jobs in their own country even though they are well trained. So they go to other countries to work and send the money they earn back home to support their families. They do everything from maintaining oil wells in the Middle East and nursing in the United States to taking care of other people's families in places like Hong Kong and Singapore.

A Hopeful Democracy

Filipinos are proud of their democratic form of government. Like its American model, the Philippines is a republic with a constitution, an elected president, and a two-house legislature: the Senate and the House of Representatives. Fidel Ramos was elected president in 1992.

The islands are divided into provinces with elected governors and provincial boards. Towns have elected mayors and councils. Even barangays (the smallest political unit) elect barangay captains.

Even so, politics in the Philippines has often been troubled and violent for many complicated reasons. Vast social and economic inequalities plus a communist guerrilla movement and a Muslim separatist rebellion are among them.

Most Filipinos, nonetheless, continue to believe in democracy. These proud, resourceful, hopeful people are struggling to make Philippine life better.

2. From Barangays to Nationhood

The Philippines has not been a nation as we know it today for most of its history. It has been independent only since 1946. The boundaries on today's maps are less than 100 years old. Yet archaeological evidence shows that people have lived on the islands for at least 40,000 years and possibly as long as 250,000 years.

Philippine history is the story of the gradual blending of the descendants of those island people and their way of life with distinctly different people and ideas that arrived much later. More than 1,000 years ago, Chinese traders linked the islanders into a wider world and introduced more complicated ways of doing business. Arabs brought Islam in the 14th century. Spanish explorers arrived over 400 years ago to colonize and convert, bringing Roman Catholicism. A century ago, the United States took over, continuing colonialism but instituting constitutional democracy.

The slow process has often been angry, bloody, and brutal. It has also been marked by patience, courage, endurance, and heroism. The result is the modern Republic of the Philippines and proud Filipinos.

Caves, Tools, Beads, and Pots

The Tabon Caves are high in a limestone cliff facing the sea on the west coast of Palawan. Tools, beads, and pottery found there tell us that, starting 40,000 years ago, many generations of people lived in the caves. Other discoveries suggest humans inhabited northern Luzon even earlier, perhaps 250,000 years ago.

Historians and archaeologists argue about these early peoples' origins. No one knows what they looked like, but they were probably small and dark. Some scholars believe that the first people to live on the islands we know today as the Philippines walked across land bridges from mainland Asia. Others believe they must have come by boat.

However they got there, by 5000 B.C. the people living in the present-day Philippines and throughout the islands of Southeast Asia had developed a common way of life. It evolved from the islanders' responses to similar geographical conditions, climate, plants, and animals. None of these ancient people had yet formed the national identities that would later be called Filipino, Malay, or Indonesian. In fact, the words they had for themselves often meant "the people."

Trade Links with China

The little we know about the early islanders suggests that

This ancient clay burial pot was discovered in a cave on the island of Palawan. The figure in the front of the boat is being transported to the world of the dead. Pots such as these tell us that people have lived on the islands for thousands of years.

even 5,000 years ago they were sailors, traveling among the islands to establish new settlements and to engage in trade. Probably as new groups of people arrived, the later arrivals married the earlier ones or pushed them inland. This process was repeated many times.

The earliest written information we have, however, comes from records kept by Chinese traders who explored the region nearly 2,000 years ago. By the seventh century A.D., and perhaps earlier, the islands were part of a complicated trading network dominated by China. Vessels from China, the rest of Southeast Asia, India, and Arabia called at the islands. Among other things, the traders were attracted by the pearls in Sulu and the cotton and fine cloth produced on Cebu.

By the tenth century, Chinese goods were everywhere in the islands. We know this from the Chinese porcelain still being unearthed from old graves. Around this time a few Chinese established coastal trading settlements.

However, the Chinese did not live in the islands in any numbers until after the Spanish came.

Datus and Barangays

Also by the tenth century, the islanders were living in isolated independent settlements of kinfolk. Groups of people had come in barangays (boats) from other places in Southeast Asia and settled throughout the islands. We do not know when this started or ended, although barangays apparently were still arriving in the 13th century. Individual settlements were made up of people who came in one boat. Therefore, *barangay* has become a word for the community. It is now used for the country's smallest political unit.

These settlements were led by a *datu* (chieftain) who could be either a man or a woman. The *datu* issued local laws, and everyone practiced elaborate manners to achieve an orderly society. These people believed in omens, spirits, and gods that could make their personal and community activities succeed or fail. Women were often religious as well as political leaders. As a sign of respect, men walked behind women.

Each family cleared a patch of forest, burned the fallen brush, and planted crops for one or two growing seasons. Then they cleared a new field elsewhere. We call this "slash-and-burn" farming. The islanders also mined, wove cloth, built boats, fished, and raised poultry and pearls. They used their own systems of weights and measures, calendars, and writing. Men and women wore cloth clothing and elaborate jewelry.

By the early 16th century, some barangays were quite large. Cebu, or Sugbu (its local name), was a thriving trading center with perhaps 300 dwellings. Maynila (now Manila) had even more.

The Coming of Islam

Arab and Indian traders and missionaries introduced Islam to the southern Philippines. Sometime in 1380 an Arabian judge, Mahdum, landed in Sulu preaching the teachings of Muhammad. In 1390, Raja Baginda, a ruler from Sumatra (in what is now Indonesia), and Abu Bakar, a trader, established the first Muslim sultanate (kingdom) of Sulu.

By the early 16th century Islam was spreading across much of Mindanao and the Visayas. Maynila, on Luzon, had also become a powerful Muslim kingdom.

Magellan and Lapulapu

Spaniards first reached the islands in 1521. Ferdinand Magellan was seeking a westward route around the world. On March 17 his three ships anchored near Samar.

Magellan planted a cross and the Spanish flag, claiming these new lands for God and king.

The ships sailed on to Sugbu. There Humabon, the local rajah (ruler), and Magellan exchanged gifts and feasted. Magellan insisted on converting the people to Christianity. He presented a carving of the Santo Niño (Christ Child) to Humabon's wife, Juana.

Magellan agreed to attack Humabon's enemy, Lapulapu, the chief of Mactan, a neighboring island. In the resulting fight, Lapulapu killed Magellan. The frightened Spaniards fled Sugbu. A year later, only one ship, under Captain Sebastian de Elcano, and 18 men returned to Spain. They had completed the first circumnavigation of the earth.

On Mactan, near where Magellan died, three monuments present completely different interpretations of the importance of these events. The oldest was erected by the Spanish in the 19th century. It glorifies God, Spain, and, only in passing, Magellan. The second, erected in 1941 during the American era, recounts the facts of Magellan's death and Elcano's completion of the circumnavigation.

The third monument, erected a decade later, reads: "Here, on 27 April 1521, Lapulapu and his men repulsed the Spanish invaders, killing their leader, Ferdinand Magellan. Thus Lapulapu became the first Filipino to have repelled European aggression."

A monument to Lapulapu, the "first Filipino to have repelled European aggression"

Conquest and Conversion

Spaniards returned to claim the islands in 1565. Miguel Lopez de Legazpi and his men landed in Sugbu and established the first permanent Spanish settlement. He found the islanders still worshiping the statue Magellan had left. Believing this was an omen, he had the first Christian church built in the islands.

As the Spaniards explored farther north, they met opposition in some places. Other places they did not. They captured Maynila on May 19, 1571.

Legazpi named the new colony Filipinas after his king, Philip II, and made Manila its capital. In less than a decade, he controlled Luzon and much of the Visayas. The Spanish king sent priests to convert the *indios* (Magellan's name for the local people). The process of unifying the islands and making them Christian had begun. However, in Sulu and Mindanao, the Moros (as the Spanish called the Muslims) resisted. There were frequent fights over the next 300 years, but the Muslims remained independent until the Americans came.

New Spain

Filipinas was "New Spain." The Spanish governor-general was virtually the king. The local people were required to pay taxes to the Spanish king and to support the Church. Male *indios* between 16 and 60 were forced to serve the government for 40 days each year. They built roads, churches, and bridges, and were sent on expeditions. This disrupted the *indios'* lives and often made the difference between good and lean harvests.

Spaniards also headed individual provinces. Many were adventurers seeking their fortunes. Former *datus* and rajahs were given official positions to keep them from resisting. Bribery and corruption were common. The friars (as priests were also called) competed with the civil officials in accumulating wealth and land. Spanish officials stayed only a short time. The friars provided the stability and continuity in the colonial government. The priest was generally the only Spaniard in a town.

Under the Bell

The conquerors believed that unless people lived in towns, education and civilization were not possible. Nor could Christianity be taught. So the friars began both to encourage and force the widely scattered islanders "under the bell," that is, to live within hearing of a church bell.

The Spaniards laid out new towns like those they left behind. Each had a plaza with a church and a municipal building. Coastal towns had forts to protect them from marauders.

The *indios* resisted resettlement. Moving to towns took them away from their livelihoods. It also changed the rhythms of their lives, which were based on the planting cycle and the weather. In town, the days were punctuated by church bells and rituals. The friars used public processions and fiestas (festivals) to encourage the *indios* to practice their new Christian faith. Establishing towns was a slow process. By the end of the 17th century, there were less than 20 villages with populations of more than 2,000.

Conversion went more rapidly. At first it was by force. But soon Catholicism was ingrained in people's

The statue of the Santo Niño, or Christ Child, that Magellan brought to the islands in 1521 is still revered today.

lives. The Latin alphabet replaced local writing forms. The friars started schools and universities for children of Spaniards. However, they discouraged teaching Spanish to *indios* since speaking it meant access to power. The *indios* changed their clothing to satisfy Spanish customs and Catholic morality. Women's positions in society also changed. The Church introduced the idea of male-only authority. Consequently, local women who had been independent were expected to defer to their fathers and husbands.

The Manila Galleons

The Manila galleons were enormous sailing ships that could hold heavy cargoes and withstand the dangers of crossing the Pacific Ocean. In the late 16th century Spain closed Filipinas to most foreign commerce except with China and Mexico. Other traders were not allowed to enter the colony's ports.

The Spanish Crown also imposed strict controls on the Manila galleons so that it would have a monopoly on Pacific trade. Only two sailings a year were allowed between the colony and Acapulco, Mexico. Loaded with goods from China, the galleons left Luzon in July or August. The voyage took about 200 days. In Mexico, the cargo was resold and shipped across the Atlantic to Spain. Galleons left Acapulco in February or March. They returned to Filipinas with Mexican silver, mail, supplies, new officials, and missionaries.

The galleon trade was the main source of income for the colonial government and for Spanish settlers. Because few local goods were involved, Spain was not interested in developing the colony. Chinese settlers controlled the trading networks that supplied the galleons. The galleon trade made little difference in the lives or incomes of the *indios.*

Open to the World

In 1762 British troops captured Manila. This humiliating Spanish defeat was one of many battles all over the world during the Seven Years War (Americans call it the French and Indian War). The British occupied Manila for two years. It was a year before news reached them that the war had ended and the colony had been returned to Spain.

The British occupation caused many changes in Filipinas. So did the Industrial Revolution, which was beginning in England at the same time. The industrial nations required more raw materials than they had. They also needed to expand their markets. So they looked to their own and other countries' colonies for both.

In 1809 a British trading company got permission to open in Manila. Six years later, when Spain opened all its colonial ports to foreign trade, the galleon monopoly ended. Soon two American companies and many European representatives came to do business.

Cash Crops and Haciendas

Until the 19th century the islanders produced things for their own use. Then outsiders came to buy their products: hemp, sugar, copra, tobacco, and coffee. Large areas of land were cleared for the first time. American and British firms provided the money.

Consequently, there was more money and prosperity in the provinces, at least for some people. Roads were built. More foreigners traveled beyond Manila, which helped lessen some of the colonial abuses.

Cash crops made owning land important. The Spanish had already declared that much of what they saw as vacant land belonged to the Church or to individuals they favored. But most of the islanders still thought land belonged to the community and could not be bought or sold. This was an ancient and basic belief of the people. The concept of private land ownership was imposed on them by the Spanish.

A few wealthy local families began accumulating land and money. They leased or bought large areas of virgin land from the friars and then rented plots to local farmers in exchange for part of each year's crop. These became the haciendas (plantations) that cover many parts of the country today.

Most of the landowning wealthy people were mestizos. Mainly, they were descendants of Chinese traders who married island women, although some had Spanish fathers. Rather than trading like the Chinese, the mestizos accumulated land. Some moved to Negros to start the sugar industry. Others cultivated indigo plants. Still others built large landholdings of rice around Manila. These families are still influential.

As people became more dependent on cash crops and money, individuals and the colony became closely tied into the ups and downs of prices around the world. Tensions rose between those with land and money and those without. These tensions still exist today.

Filipinos and *Ilustrados*

During the early Spanish period the term *Filipinos* referred to Spaniards born in Filipinas. But by the mid-19th century, life in Filipinas was changing rapidly. Many islanders were thinking of themselves in new ways.

By then many mestizo families were in the fourth or fifth generation. They were aware that they were not clearly Chinese or Spanish or *indio.* Yet they knew they belonged to the islands. At the same time, many islanders felt the term *indio,* which the Spanish used for them, was insulting. So the mestizos and islanders began using *Filipino* to mean people born in the islands no matter what their race, religion, or ancestry.

In 1863 the Spanish introduced education reforms in the islands. They opened the universities to non-Spaniards. As a result, many mestizos could educate their children. Known as *ilustrados,* these highly educated young people began to resent Spanish rule and to develop a strong sense of Filipino nationalism. Along with the sense of pride in their nation came the conviction that the country should rule itself.

Resistance and Rebellion

Ever since the Spanish had arrived, groups of islanders had rebelled somewhere in the colony every five or six years. The Spanish forcibly put down these uprisings.

However, the British occupation of Manila in 1762 showed the islanders that their conquerors could be beaten.

During and after the British occupation there were two years of widespread upheaval. As part of that, Diego Silang declared that his native Ilocos in northern Luzon was free. When he offered to help the British the Church turned some of the people against him. Silang was assassinated. His wife, Gabriela, continued the revolt. Eventually, she and the small army she led were captured and executed.

A century later the colony was ripe for revolution. Filipinos were angry because few of them could hope for important positions. Laborers at the Cavite arsenal in Luzon revolted. Although the uprising was quickly stopped, Spanish authorities arrested individuals on charges of treason. Among them were three Filipino priests, Fathers José Burgos, Jacinto Zamora, and Mariano Gomez. There was no evidence that the priests were involved. Even so, they were martyred on February 17, 1872. Active Filipino nationalism can be dated from that morning.

Within a decade the Spanish authorities in Filipinas were exiling some *ilustrados* because of their nationalist ideas. Others escaped to Spain and elsewhere in Europe. In Spain they organized the Propagandists, a group that wrote papers advocating Filipino equality. The Spanish saw them as enemies of Spain and the Church.

José Rizal is the most famous Propagandist. Sometimes he is called the "George Washington of the Philippines." His novels gave an unflattering picture of Philippine life under Spanish rule and advocated reforms and separation from Spain. Church authorities in Manila banned his first novel, *Noli Me Tangere* (Touch Me Not). This only increased the book's secret readership and spread its nationalistic ideas.

The Revolution Begins

At the same time, in the Philippines, Andrés Bonifacio was organizing the Katipunan, the Society of the Sons of the People. This secret society distributed underground newspapers and collected arms and money in an attempt to gain independence.

Bonifacio was an office worker, not an *ilustrado*. The revolutionary language he used frightened many of the *ilustrados* he wanted to recruit, including Rizal. On August 26, 1896, Bonifacio called for Filipinos to rebel. Many *ilustrados* did not join the rebellion that spread through the Manila area. The revolutionary forces were defeated in their first battle three days later. Nonetheless, the governor-general declared a state of war in eight provinces around Manila.

The Spanish tried Rizal, who by this time had returned to the Philippines, even though he had not been part of the rebellion. On December 30, 1896, he was publicly shot in Manila. The execution of Rizal convinced the people that there was no justice.

Another revolutionary, Emilio Aguinaldo, believed an elected government should replace the Katipunan. He issued a statement declaring that the revolution's aim was Philippine independence with a new government similar to that of the United States. Bonifacio believed the Katipunan should govern. On March 22, 1897, the revolutionaries met and elected Aguinaldo president. Bonifacio left in a rage. He and his brother were caught by Aguinaldo's men and executed.

The governor-general finally realized that as soon as he crushed Filipino forces in one place, they sprang up in another. So he tried to settle with Aguinaldo and managed to convince the rebel leader to leave the country with his life and the promise of a sum of money. Aguinaldo and his companions went to Hong Kong and continued the revolutionary government from there.

Battle of Manila Bay

Again events far away influenced changes in the Philippines. The United States was producing more goods than it could consume and needed to expand its markets, so it was looking at Asia. Cuba, another of Spain's colonies, was revolting. The relationship between

Spain and the United States was steadily worsening.

In December 1897, American President William McKinley pressured Spain into granting Cuba limited self-government. The Cuban rebels continued fighting. The battleship USS *Maine* was sent to Cuba to protect American citizens. It exploded there. An angry American public blamed Spain. On April 25, 1898, the United States declared war on Spain.

Admiral George Dewey, commander of the United States Asiatic Squadron, as it was called then, was ordered to Manila. On May 1, 1898, his fleet entered Manila Bay and destroyed the Spanish fleet there. The Battle of Manila Bay was the first important battle of the Spanish-American War. Dewey's victory thrilled Americans. It also sent them scurrying to maps. Most Americans did not know where the Philippine islands were.

Aguinaldo Returns

The Filipino struggle for freedom began again. Aguinaldo returned to Manila and met with Dewey. According to Aguinaldo, Dewey told him the Americans did not want colonies. Dewey later denied this. He claimed he had extended the formal honors due a general to Aguinaldo personally rather than officially. Therefore, Aguinaldo may have mistaken the American government's position.

On June 12, 1898, Aguinaldo issued a Declaration of

Independence. The present Republic of the Philippines dates its independence from that declaration. By the end of June, most of Luzon was in rebel hands except for Manila and the nearby port of Cavite, which the Spanish still held.

Dewey blockaded Manila Bay to keep supplies from getting to the city. Aguinaldo surrounded Manila by land, withholding food and water. The Spanish would not give up. To them, surrendering, especially to the Filipinos, meant a loss of honor.

Dewey made a secret agreement with the Spanish so that they could lose honorably. He agreed to keep Aguinaldo's forces out and to fight a mock battle for Manila on August 13. Dewey did not know that an armistice with Spain had been signed the previous day.

In the Treaty of Paris, which ended the war, Spain granted Cuba its independence but gave Guam, Puerto Rico, and the Philippines to the United States in exchange for $20 million. The Filipinos contended that the islands were not Spain's to give, but no one listened.

Controversy also raged in the United States. Many Americans did not like their new position as a colonial power. This feeling was so strong that the Treaty of Paris was ratified in the U.S. Senate by only a one-vote margin.

The Philippine-American War

President McKinley declared that while the U.S. military

government would establish services to improve the life of Filipinos, it would assume sovereignty over the entire country, by force if necessary.

The outraged Filipinos believed the Americans had promised them immediate independence. Filipino leaders proclaimed the Philippine Republic with Aguinaldo as president. Sixty delegates met in Malolos outside of Manila to draft a constitution. On January 21, 1899, Aguinaldo announced the Malolos Constitution. Then Filipinos continued fighting for their new republic.

Americans know little about the Philippine-American war, which lasted over two years. Many of the clashes were guerrillalike, brutal, and bloody. Thousands of taos (peasants) died in the cause for independence to which tens of thousands of Filipinos were committed. According to writings at the time, American soldiers engaged in cruelties that were more severe than anything done by the Spanish.

As the Americans maintained control, important Filipino leaders began slipping away from the independence movement. They saw that they were losing and were tempted by the American offers of jobs within the new colonial government. Ordinary Filipinos who were making maximum sacrifices for independence felt abandoned. It was 1902 before the last Filipinos surrendered.

At the same time, the United States Marines were

fighting the Moro Wars. For the first time the fiercely independent Muslims were defeated. They have been part of the Philippines ever since, and the Philippines gained its present boundaries.

American Rule

In 1901 the United States established a government with an American governor-general and a five-man commission to rule the Philippine islands, as the new colony was called. This government was intended to prepare Filipinos for eventual self-rule. William Howard Taft (later president of the United States) was the first governor-general.

The American colonial government sold the last of the estates held by the Church to leading Filipinos. This strengthened the oligarchy, a ruling group of a few wealthy families. It also widened the division between the wealthy and poor that had begun under the Spanish.

The Americans built roads and began basic sanitation and health services. But the United States' best legacy to the Philippines was widespread public education in English for both boys and girls.

The Americans introduced democratic institutions based on their own. National elections were held for the first time in 1907. Local officials and members of the first Philippine Assembly were elected. Filipinos also elected two nonvoting representatives to the U.S. House of

Representatives. Women obtained the right to vote in 1937. They have played active roles in Philippine public life and politics ever since.

In 1934 the American Congress enacted the Tydings-McDuffie Act. It made the Philippines a commonwealth (a self-governing territory within the United States) for ten years, beginning in 1935. Total independence would follow. In 1935, Manuel Quezon was elected the first Commonwealth president. Sergio Osmeña was his vice president.

World War II

On December 8 (Manila time), 1941, the Japanese bombed Manila after they bombed Pearl Harbor in Hawaii. World War II had begun for the Philippines and the United States. The Japanese invaded the Philippines. Philippine and American troops under General Douglas MacArthur fought valiantly but were overwhelmed. American President Franklin Roosevelt ordered General MacArthur to leave for Australia. As MacArthur left, he promised, "I shall return."

Thousands of the Fil-Am soldiers, as they were called, were captured. The Japanese forced them to make a grueling march in the Bataan Peninsula on Luzon. So many died that this is called the Bataan "Death March." Japanese rule was harsh. Everyone suffered. Most Filipinos resisted. A courageous guerrilla movement fought throughout the islands. They fought partly on behalf of the Americans. But most of all, it was their own war. The Japanese threatened Philippine independence.

In October 1944, MacArthur kept his promise. Osmeña, who had become president in Washington when Quezon died there in exile, waded ashore with MacArthur. As the troops advanced through the islands, what had not been destroyed during the Japanese occupation was flattened in the American liberation. Manila was especially devastated in fierce house-to-house fighting.

Republic of the Philippines

The Republic of the Philippines became independent on July 4, 1946. Manuel Roxas was its first president. The fledgling nation faced many problems.

It needed to rebuild its economic life. Aid from the United States was less than Filipinos expected. Nonetheless, because of prewar business ties, parts of the Philippine economy remained closely linked to the United States. Rebuilding provided many money-making opportunities. Manila began to rise from the rubble. Ordinary folk flocked to the cities in search of work.

In central Luzon, many dissatisfied peasants joined the Communist-led Hukbalahap movement, commonly known as the Huks. Most Huks were tenant farmers with long-standing grievances over land they thought rightfully belonged to them. The Huks soon controlled large portions of Luzon. Although the movement was broken up in the early 1950s, the basic problems of land ownership remained.

In 1953 Ramon Magsaysay became the first non-*ilustrado* president. Surrounded by capable and dedicated Filipinos, he began developing the countryside. Perhaps like no other leader, he understood the concerns of Filipinos. Unfortunately, before his term ended, he was killed in a plane crash.

Relations with the United States

After independence, the Philippines' relationship with the United States remained complex. American fads, slang, movies, and products were popular. Some Filipinos wanted the country to be an American state. Others felt that America dominated too much of Philippine life. Over the years, Philippine currency, the peso, was separated from the U.S. dollar. Many American special rights ended, although American companies continued to do business there.

The prickliest difficulty was the prewar military bases the United States had kept. The major ones were Clark Field Air Base and Subic Bay Naval Base, both in Luzon. Because of them the American government became the second-largest employer in the Philippines.

Periodically the two countries discussed changes in the agreements that let the United States use the bases. The big issues were the amount of money the Americans should pay for their use and how much control the Philippines would have. Filipino nationalists believed that until the Americans left the bases, the Philippines could not be entirely free. Many other Filipinos wanted the Americans to stay.

From Marcos to Aquino

Ferdinand Marcos was elected president in 1965. Four years later, he became the first Filipino president to be reelected for a second full term. Just before that term ended, he suspended the constitution and declared martial law in 1972. This meant he remained president but stopped the democratic process.

By 1984 most of the country had gotten poorer while the president and his friends had grown wealthier. There were about 20,000 Communist-led guerrillas all over the country. In addition, Muslims in Mindanao were fighting to gain self-government. Most Filipinos were disgusted with President Marcos and afraid of the Communists. Filipinos began demonstrating in the streets.

Finally Marcos called a special presidential election for February 7, 1986. Corazon Aquino, called "Cory," ran

against him. Everyone voted, although they were afraid
of Marcos's henchmen. Most people thought Cory won.
But Marcos controlled the official ballot counting and
said she did not.

Two weeks later, part of the Philippine military
mutinied. The people of Manila joined them and filled the
streets to block Marcos's tanks. President Marcos and his
wife, Imelda, fled the country. Mrs. Aquino was sworn in
as president.

President Aquino set out to reestablish democracy.
Her government wrote and ratified a new constitution.
Filipinos elected a new government. But during her six
years as president, things did not go as well as everyone
hoped. Filipinos in and out of government argued about
what to do. Few services had improved. Not only were the
guerrillas still fighting, but some military officers tried to
overthrow Aquino's government several times.

The American military base issue was finally settled
in 1991. While a new agreement was being discussed,
Mount Pinatubo erupted. The ash destroyed Clark Field
Air Base, so the United States closed it. The Philippine
Senate rejected the agreement the American and Philippine
governments had reached. The United States left Subic
Bay in November 1992. The departure of the American
forces created an opportunity for the two countries to
establish a new relationship.

In May 1992, Fidel Ramos was elected president.

President Corazon Aquino restored constitutional government to the Philippines after 20 years of dictatorship under Ferdinand Marcos.

The country's problems remain. The future will not be easy. But as the Philippines nears the hundredth anniversary of its Declaration of Independence, Filipinos continue to strive. Their proud heritage has brought them from isolated barangays to nationhood.

3. Making It All Filipino

Josechu and Ramonito straddle the broad back of the family carabao (water buffalo). The boys ride it up the path from the rice fields toward their small house built on stilts. Riding the carabao home is their nightly chore, as it is for boys all over the rural Philippines. When they are free, the brothers catch spiders to use in the spiderfights they and their *barkada* (gangmates) enjoy.

Every Sunday after mass, Fely and her sisters, brothers, and cousins go to their grandparents' house in Manila. The first thing they do is find their Lola (grandmother) and Lolo (grandfather) to *mano po:* Fely touches Lola's and Lolo's hands to her own forehead. She does this both as a courtesy to them and a blessing for herself. Then the children go off to play Nintendo.

Nabanal wears a T-shirt and jeans like many of his teenage friends. Since leaving school, Nabanal and his friends are working on building the new road high in the mountains of northern Luzon. He is not interested in learning how his uncle Natido trims narrow rattan strips to plait a *bongo*. (A *bongo* is a backpack basket that by community custom only men may carry.)

A little girl greets her grandmother in the traditional way.

His uncle is the village *mumbaki,* a leader who performs traditional healing ceremonies, weddings, and funerals and serves as the community peacemaker.

Each Friday, the loudspeaker at the mosque in Marawi, a small town in northern Mindanao, sounds the call to prayer just as mosques do all over the Muslim world. Ali hurries after his father and the other faithful as they gather for the main worship of the week.

Nita has finished school and needs a job. Early one morning, her father takes her to the mayor's house to ask him to help her find one. The mayor is her father's compadre (godfather): The mayor stood sponsor at Nita's parents' wedding and has a familylike obligation to help her.

Bouncing her little brother on her hip, Sol packs the sweet yellow mangoes Cebu is famous for into the flat round basket. The next morning, with her mother, she will carry them down the steep hill to sell by the roadside.

Iking runs along the divider in the middle of Manila's bustling Roxas Boulevard. When the light turns red, he darts into the traffic to peddle cigarettes one at a time to people in the stopped cars. His meager earnings help pay his little sisters' school fees.

At dawn on the morning of the annual barrio fiesta (village celebration), Bebe picks flowers from the garden. Her aunt will use them to decorate the *carroza* (hand-drawn cart) that will carry the statue of our Lady in the procession around the barrio.

Both the Same and Different

The daily lives of each of these young people both differ greatly and have much in common. Philippine history provides some of the reasons for this. On the one hand, the majority of people share a common culture that predates the long period of Western rule. Like their distant ancestors, modern Filipinos believe in the importance of social harmony, strong extended families, and respect for elders. On the other hand, Spanish and American influences have been strong and have contributed to the diversity of the people.

Geography has played perhaps the greatest role in making the nation a patchwork of cultures. The fact that the Philippines is a nation of islands and mountains helps explain a lot. While the majority of Filipinos are lowlanders, their customs, daily language, and ways of earning a living vary from area to area. The people in Bicol (on the southern end of Luzon), for example, eat spicier food than most Filipinos. Visayans eat corn every day rather than rice. Steep, rocky Ilocos (in northern Luzon) is a difficult place in which to earn a living. Negros Oriental (eastern Negros) has a large fertile plain, so living there is easier.

The many ways Filipinos think about themselves and one another grow out of these differences. "Cebuanos (people from Cebu) are easygoing," they will say. Or "Ilocanos (from Ilocos) are hardworking and thrifty." Or "The women from Pampanga (in central Luzon) are good cooks but their men are spoiled." These generalizations are about as valid as observations Americans make about southerners, northerners, easterners, or westerners.

Nine languages are spoken among the majority of people. Three are widely used: Cebuano, in much of the Visayas and northern Mindanao, and Tagalog and Ilocano in central and northern Luzon. While all Philippine languages are in the same family, with many similar words, each is unique. If you speak Cebuano, you cannot understand Tagalog unless you learn it. Imagine living in New York and not being able to understand people in Atlanta.

Filipinos proudly identify themselves as Filipinos to outsiders. But to one another, they identify themselves by their home province and town. Each community is proud of its local heritage. When they move to big cities in the Philippines or live in other countries, Filipinos often gather in smaller groups based on the locality they come from and the language they speak.

Philippine society also divides between the poor, mostly rural mass and the tiny group of almost all-powerful wealthy families. In between are growing numbers of people who earn their livings in small businesses and as professionals—doctors, lawyers, teachers, and architects. Whether they live in the countryside, like Josechu and Ramonito, a town, or one of the big cities, like Fely, also makes many differences. So does the amount of education people have.

Isolated Cultural Minorities

Many cultural minorities, often descendants of the Philippines' first inhabitants, are scattered throughout the islands. Each group is isolated in its own place, with its own rich traditions, crafts, clothes, music, language, and religious beliefs. Many of these groups are animists, people who worship spirits they believe are in all things.

Most minority groups are uplanders, living in the mountains. Some still practice slash-and-burn farming. The Ifugao people, to which Nabanal and his uncle belong, are one of the larger groups of uplanders. But with their ancient rice terraces, they are settled farmers.

Other ethnic minorities live along rivers or shallow seas. Until recently, for instance, the Bajau, often called "sea gypsies," spent most of their lives on small boats in the waters around the numerous islands of the Sulu Archipelago. Now many of them live in settlements on land.

As more roads are built and these groups of people become less isolated, many of their traditional ways are

An Ifugao farmer surveys his land.

changing. The children go to the same kinds of schools
other Filipino children do. Radios also bring in new ideas
and link people to the rest of the country. Young people
like Nabanal are not always interested in keeping or even
learning the old ways.

Spanish, English, and Pilipino

During their 300-year rule, the Spaniards made little
effort to teach islanders their language. Educated, Spanish-
speaking Filipinos—the *ilustrados*—were an extremely
small group. Today, a few Filipinos still speak Spanish.
More importantly, many Spanish words have become
everyday words in the major Philippine languages: *barrio,
calesa, compadre,* and *fiesta,* for instance.

After the Americans took over the country in 1898,
they introduced English. English is used for government,
big business, and higher education. Almost anywhere
you go, you find lots of people who speak it fluently
with a distinctive lilt and the latest American slang. In
fact, the Philippines is the world's third-largest English-
speaking country.

The national language is not any of these, however.
It is Pilipino. The Commonwealth government created
Pilipino in 1938 in an effort to unify the country. It is
based mainly on Tagalog. Most Filipinos now speak
Pilipino as a second language. Unless they are Tagalog

speakers, however, they use something else every day.

Religion and Names

The Philippines prides itself on being the only predominantly Christian country in Asia. Nine Filipinos out of ten are Christian, as their ancestors before them have been for 400 years. Most, like the Spaniards who converted them, are Roman Catholic. In this century, American missionaries introduced various Protestant denominations. Fely's family's regular attendance at mass and Bebe's excitement about getting things ready for the barrio fiesta reflect ways Catholic observances shape Philippine daily life.

As the Spaniards converted the local people, they gave them Christian first names that were actually Spanish. The indigenous people did not have last names until 1844, when the Spanish governor-general decreed they must adopt them. For that purpose, he provided the provincial leaders with a list of names taken from the Spanish tax rolls.

That is why many Filipinos today have Hispanic given names like Juan, Corazon, Ferdinand, or Maria and family names like Marcos, Natividad, Pelaez, or Fernandez. Filipinos just cannot leave names alone, however. They give everyone a nickname: Jun, Cory, Ding, Baby, Boy, Bong-bong, Ramonito—"little Ramon."

A mosque in southern Mindanao, the part of the Philippines where most of the inhabitants are Muslims

Today, Muslims like Ali are a minority, about 5 percent of all Filipinos. But they are a majority where they live, in the southern part of Mindanao and the Sulu Archipelago. Muslim Filipinos often have names like Ali that are found throughout the Islamic world.

Filipino Chinese have adopted many local customs while retaining many of their own traditions. Most speak Philippine languages and English. Within the family and their businesses, many still speak Chinese. A number are devout Christians, but not all. Temples for traditional Chinese Buddhist and Taoist worship are found in Chinese communities. Many Chinese have retained their family names—Lee or Lim, for instance. But they often use Christian first names.

Unifying Values: Family and Loyalty

Values shared by all Filipinos bridge their many differences. Maintaining close family ties is the central value. Families, however, are not just parents and children. They are whole clans of Lolos, Lolas, parents, children, Titas (aunts), Titos (uncles), and cousins. Clans are then connected to one another by compadres (godfathers) and comadres (godmothers). Godparents are usually friends or important members of the community who are asked to sponsor babies at baptisms and couples at weddings. In doing so, they become like members of the family.

Loyalty is highly valued. It is owed above all to members of the family. Then, in ever-widening circles, it is extended to the compadre and comadre and their families, to friends and schoolmates, and finally to other people from the same community.

The debt of gratitude is the other side of loyalty. Do someone even a little favor and the person remembers forever. Filipinos are extremely careful to pay back favors done for them by others. To say that someone is without shame and careless in paying back favors is one of the worst things that can be said about a Filipino. As they play together, Josechu, Ramonito, and their *barkada* are building the links for a lifetime of being able to count on one another for help.

Likewise, when the mayor agreed to be a sponsor at Nita's parents' wedding, he knew that as a result he could count on them to help him. Their whole family would vote for him at election time, for example. He also expected that Nita's family would ask if they needed something, like a job for Nita.

Shame, Respect, and *Bahala na*

When Nita's father asks the favor, he does not necessarily do it directly. He may say he has brought Nita to pay her respects to the mayor since she has just finished school. What is needed—the job—may only be hinted at. Or it may be asked for in an extremely quiet voice. If the favor a Filipino wants is difficult to grant, someone else may be sent to ask for it. For Filipinos, it is important not to put other people in the position of having to say no to them directly. Both people would be shamed. Shaming someone else, particularly in public, is a terrible insult.

From the time they are little, Filipinos are taught to respect their elders. That is why Fely goes first to her Lola and Lolo before she goes off to play. The responsibility to care for younger people is the other side of respect. That is why Iking uses the money he earns to help his younger sisters through school. It is also why Sol carries her

Young people forge friendships that last a lifetime.

brother around as she helps her mother.

Filipinos work hard and want to get ahead. But they also believe that life is outside their control. What happens is in the hands of God: *Bahala na* (what happens, happens). Before a big exam, besides studying, many students light candles at church. When they pass, they light others in gratitude.

For Filipinos, acting according to these values helps to keep relationships between people harmonious. When there are tensions and disagreements, such behavior at least keeps the surface smooth. And that is a most Filipino virtue.

4. Stories and Legends: How Things Came to Be

Filipinos enjoy telling stories and, in turn, their stories tell us a lot about them.

Many of their myths and legends are from the time before the coming of Islam, the Spanish, and Christianity. No one knows how long ago these stories were first told. As Filipinos accepted beliefs from worldwide religions, they blended these new ideas into the older tales. And they added new stories.

Why Tell Stories?

Through the ancient tellings, the elders taught the young how things came to be, how the universe is ordered, how humans should behave, how good struggles with evil. The stories often describe a world with many spirits: for rice, the sea, streams, trees, rocks, and animals. There are mythical beasts and dangerous ghosts.

Above these spirits, the stories tell us, is a supreme creator who is as constant as the sun, yet very human. Like the many languages of the people, this creator has many names.

Each group within the Philippines has its own stories,

told in its own language. Epics—long, carefully memorized tales—are chanted for special occasions by some groups. They are carefully taught to the next generation. They often celebrate events and heroes that strengthen historical pride. Some stories simply amuse and delight. Knowing the stories helps people have a common cultural identity.

Most are part of a centuries-old spoken, or oral, tradition. They come from a time before electric lights, radios, and books, when people told stories around the fire. These stories survive because grandparents told them to grandchildren who then told them to their grandchildren.

As smaller groups of Filipinos became integrated into the wider Pilipino—or English-educated—communities, their stories were not always passed on to the younger generations. Life changed. People got busier and had less time to tell stories. Sometimes, parents or children were embarrassed by the old stories because they were not "modern" enough. Stories like Little Red Riding Hood were taught in schools. Now, TV and video—with Popeye, Big Bird, and the Teenage Mutant Ninja Turtles—have become the national storytellers.

Even so, the ancient stories live. Students read them in school. Philippine movies enact their legendary struggles between good and evil. And many grandparents continue to tell them.

Ancient stories are told to children by elders, like this grandmother of the Ifugao tribe.

The stories that follow are just a few of the many kinds found in the Philippines. The first two, told in many versions throughout the islands, are about Filipinos' origins and their pride in their brownness. The third recounts the beginnings of local customs and beliefs.

Just Right

In the beginning, God formed the first person just like a cook makes a cookie. Then God put the person on the fire to bake. But God got busy and left the person on too long. That person came out all burned and black.

So God tried again. This time, God took the person out too soon and the person was underdone and white.

The third time, the person came out of the fire all brown, beautiful, and just right—like the Filipino.

si **Malakas** *at si* **Maganda**

Before time began, the world was empty. It was Bathalang Maykapal's home, and he was alone in its nothingness. But with nothing to see or hear, he became lonely.

So he raised his arm and swung it across the void, making the sun shine warm and golden and the sky fill with puffy clouds. A round moon shimmered and stars dotted the night.

Then Bathalang Maykapal raised another arm. And behold, there was the earth, a paradise with soaring trees, grass, fragrant flowers, and singing birds. As his deputies, Bathalang Maykapal made a ruler for each of the families of creatures.

One day, the king of the birds, his giant white wings glistening in the sunlight, soared over the trees in a wide circle. He saw tall bamboo swaying in the breeze and landed there to rest.

Tak. Tak. A knocking sound came from inside the bamboo. Then the bird heard a muffled voice.

"Free us, O mighty king of birds. With your strong beak, break the bamboo imprisoning us."

Is this a trap? the great bird wondered. Suddenly, a lizard slithered up the bamboo. How hungry the bird felt. He pecked at the lizard. And missed. So the giant bird pecked again. Hard.

Crack. The bamboo split open. Out stepped a strong man and a beautiful woman. And so it was that women and men stepped into the world together and equal.

"Thank you, O great king of birds. I am Malakas," said the man. "This is Maganda, my wife. You have freed us, king of birds, and we are grateful. Come live with us."

"No," replied the king of birds. "The sky is my home. I fly with the wind. My wings are for sailing the air. But I will always sing for you and the many children and grandchildren you will have. My birdlings will fly around you, singing my songs. Come. Ride on my back and I will show you your homeland."

As they circled the wide world, they saw a cluster of islands, green and lovely under the sun, sparkling like precious emeralds in the sea. And so it was that in the beautiful islands Malakas and Maganda, the Strong and the Beautiful, made a home for the brown race.

Apo Babowa

Ba-i Babowa was a faithful wife to a farmer, according to the Maranao people of Mindanao. Every day at noon, she went to the fields with food for her hardworking husband.

"Do not bring me food anymore, faithful wife," the farmer told her. "From now on, I will eat lunch at home." And he did.

One day, he did not come. She waited until dark, but still he did not appear. So Ba-i Babowa called all her relatives in the village. They lit torches and rushed to the field to look for him.

When they got there, all they found was the carabao tied to a sapling. The villagers searched until they reached a huge tree inhabited by spirits.

"Your husband must have been enchanted by the spirits and made invisible," the frightened relatives told Ba-i Babowa. "Let's burn down the tree."

But before they could, the husband spoke. "Do not harm me, faithful wife. I am in here safe. But from now on, no farmer can clear the field without making an offering to me. In return, I will protect the crops from pests and calamities." And so it is, even today.

Although Ba-i Babowa went home, she could not be consoled. Finally, she decided to throw herself in the Agus River. Before she did, she declared, "From now on, I shall be the guardian of mothers. Those who descend from me must invite me to the blessing of their children. In return, I will protect their babies from illness." Which is why even now, on the seventh day after their birth, Maranao children are anointed with water brought from the river.

5. Fiesta: Time to Celebrate

Filipinos love fiestas. These celebrations give meaning to their lives and rhythm to their years. They combine worship, food, music, and often spectacle and dance. Families and communities gather together. Many members come back from cities far away or even from overseas to participate.

Different communities celebrate in different ways. Each small group that still lives according to the ancient ways has its own rituals and festivals. Muslim Filipinos celebrate the cycle of festivals common to the Islamic world. Most Filipinos observe Christian holidays. Because they were introduced by Spanish Roman Catholics, the majority of Filipino traditions are similar to those practiced throughout the Spanish-speaking world. Even though the origins of many of these festivals are foreign, they have become distinctly Filipino.

Many Different Years

Festivals are a way of marking the year. However, not all Filipinos count the number of days in a year in the same way. The Christian calendar, used internationally, is the official calendar of the Philippines. It is solar, based on

All dressed up for fiesta

the 365 days it takes the earth to rotate around the sun. In the Philippines, the dates of Christian holidays are added in a cycle determined by the Church.

Muslim holidays follow the worldwide Islamic year. It is lunar, based on the moon's 354-day rotation around the earth. The year has 12 months, from new moon to new moon. Six months are 29 days long; six months are 30 days long. Days go from sundown to sundown. The first day of the Christian year (January 1) and the first day of the Muslim year (1 Muharram) fall on the same day only once every 32 years. Friday rather than Sunday is the main day of weekly worship for Muslims.

Perhaps the most unusual year is observed by the Ifugao, the builders of the famous rice terraces in the mountains of Luzon. Their year is based on the rice-growing cycle rather than on the movements of the sun, earth, and moon. Furthermore, the number of days a year in each of the region's four agricultural districts differs slightly. Each reflects its area's own height, climate, and the stages of growing rice. One year does not usually have the exact number of days as the one before or after it, either. Each is more or less a solar year, however.

Rice and Sacred Days of Rest

The Ifugao's major festivals are based on the four rice-growing seasons. The many rituals accompanying each one are as much a part of growing rice as the work itself. The cycle starts with the off-season (roughly August to November) when the Ifugao repair the terraces and ready the pond-fields. The planting season (December to March) follows. Then comes the dry season (April to about mid-June), the time for weeding. The cycle ends with the harvest (late June to July).

Community rituals take place during *tengao,* or "sacred rest days." These days are set by the council of elders when they think the time is right. For the most important rituals, a whole district is marked off to keep people from entering or leaving it. Community leaders make offerings of food to the ancestors, local spirits, and hundreds of gods. Chickens, pigs, or, on extremely special occasions, carabao are killed as sacrifices. Gongs and drums are beaten. Incantations (words believed to have special powers) are chanted. Each small stage in the rice cycle has its own ritual.

Planting and harvesting are especially important. The person chosen to plant the first field hosts that ceremony for the whole community. Harvest is homecoming time. This is also the period for brewing rice beer, drinking, feasting, dancing, and courting. Many animals are sacrificed. The leaders who conduct rituals bring out the carved statues that protect the granaries. Throughout the harvest, everyone works together, going from field to field. During the last four days of the season the Ifugao celebrate the end of one cycle and the beginning of the next. They chant their myths, return the statues to their places, store the harvest, and close the granary doors.

Hari Raya

For Muslim Filipinos, *hari raya* means "big day." One of the most important holidays for Muslims, *Hari Raya* comes after Ramadan, the ninth month.

Every day in Ramadan, Muslims are required to fast from dawn until sunset. The faithful—even schoolchildren—do not eat, drink, smoke, or do other pleasurable things during these hours. When the imam (Muslim religious leader) sees the tenth new moon, he declares the end of Ramadan and the end of the fast. The next morning, the faithful go to the mosque for prayers. Everyone begs forgiveness and forgives in return. Feasting and merrymaking then begin.

In Lanao Province in northern Mindanao, young men go around at dawn beating gongs and drums. The *datu* (headman) leads a procession through the community, escorted by dancers, musicians, men on horseback. At home, families feast on highly spiced food, yellow rice, and cakes of all kinds. The rest of the day everyone visits friends, eats more, and watches traditional sports. Children receive gifts.

Muslim Filipinos observe two other major festivals

and many minor ones. Hari Raya Haji, the tenth day of the twelfth month, marks the time Muslims are commanded, if they are able, to make the haji, the pilgrimage to Mecca. It also commemorates God's testing of the faith of Abraham, when he ordered him to sacrifice his son. Muslims sacrifice goats and cattle, sharing the meat with the poor. Religious processions and feasting mark *Maolod en Nabi,* the Prophet Muhammad's birthday, on the twelfth day of the second month.

The Christmas Season

Filipinos often say they celebrate the longest Christmas season in the world. The store decorations that go up in October would be familiar to people in the United States. Sound systems blare seasonal music, Santa Clauses appear, and trees are decorated. Midnight mass and family gatherings on Christmas Day are the center of the holiday. The Feast of the Three Kings on January 6 ends the season.

For the nine days prior to Christmas, before dawn each morning, church bells call worshipers to early-morning mass. This novena (nine-day cycle of masses) is called *misa de gallo.*

Throughout the season, groups of children and grownups go from house to house caroling in return for gifts of food and money. Sometimes they walk. Often they ride a jeepney—a long jeep—and sing into a microphone. In addition to folk melodies and local versions of Spanish carols, they also sing songs like "White Christmas" and "Rudolph the Red-nosed Reindeer."

Houses are decorated with *farol,* star-shaped lanterns made of bamboo sticks covered with colored paper. In small villages, these hang in the windows of each of the wooden houses. In bigger towns, many houses are decorated with bright strings of electric lights.

The residents of each section of San Fernando, the capital of Pampanga (in central Luzon), and many surrounding communities mount huge, spectacularly lit lanterns on trucks. On Christmas Eve, at around nine o'clock, the trucks roll through town. They gather in the town plaza where, after the midnight mass, the lanterns are judged.

Lent and Holy Week

Lent, from Ash Wednesday to Easter Sunday, is a somber season. In many communities the older people take turns chanting from their old copies of the *Pasión* (the life and death of Christ) as told in the local languages. In Ilocos, in the far north of Luzon, the old women wail like they do for the *dung-aw,* or traditional lament for the dead that predates Christianity.

Palm Sunday starts Holy Week. Filipinos weave palm fronds into elaborate designs. They take them to church

During Holy Week, some Christian communities hold processions that reenact the crucifixion.

to wave as a remembrance of Christ's triumphal entry into Jerusalem. After mass, the priest blesses the palms. The faithful hang the palms above their doors and windows in the belief they will keep the householders safe.

Religious processions are held after dark on Holy Monday and Holy Thursday before Easter. Men and older boys take turns pulling huge floats, called *carrozas,* through the streets. These carry scenes recalling the events of the *Pasión.* Sometimes people act out the story. Life-size wooden statues—often hundreds of years old— are also used to tell the story.

On Good Friday penitents dressed in brown robes and crowns of leaves walk barefoot through the streets, dragging heavy wooden crosses on their shoulders. In some areas, people called *flagellantes* strip to the waist and beat their backs with ropes until they are raw. In a few places, the faithful reenact Christ's crucifixion by suspending themselves from standing crosses. The Church condemns the more gruesome of these practices. Even so, the spectacles draw large crowds.

Visitors come to Marinduque, south of Luzon, from all over to witness the Morion Festival held on Easter. The festival reenacts the legend of the Roman centurion Longinus, who was blind in one eye. His sight, according to tradition, was miraculously restored by a drop of Christ's blood. The other centurions killed Longinus for proclaiming his newfound belief. *Morion* means "mask" or "visor." Townsmen make enormous centurion masks and wear them for ceremonies throughout Holy Week.

All Saints' Day

On All Saints' Day, November 1, Filipinos remember their dead, clean the graves, and decorate them with

Centurion masks are worn as part of the Easter celebrations in Marinduque.

flowers. While the purpose is somber, the effect is a picnic, full of merrymaking and laughter. Everyone goes to the cemetery. The roads are jammed. Each family takes lots of food for themselves and their friends. At night, they turn on elaborate lights put up for the occasion.

Everyone also goes visiting from one family plot to another within the cemetery, leaving flowers and lighting candles on the graves of relatives and friends, chatting with one another and eating. In this way they reinforce bonds that go back generations.

Barrio Fiestas

Every city, town, and barrio has its own patron saint. The saints' days are traditionally celebrated with a fiesta. In addition to a procession in which the people accompany the saint's image through the area, these fiestas feature singing, dancing, and lots of food. Many families keep open house, with long tables filled with special dishes. Everyone goes from house to house, visiting friends and eating everywhere they stop. Some places hold a beauty pageant to choose a fiesta queen.

Among the oldest saints' day fiestas are those that honor the Santo Niño, or Holy Child. The Sinulug in Cebu, held on the third weekend each January, is one of the most important. The statue of the Santo Niño that Magellan brought to Cebu is still there. After 450 years,

Filipinos light candles for many occasions, including All Saints' Day.

it remains an object of devotion. Even though Cebu has suffered many fires and earthquakes and was bombed flat in World War II, the Santo Niño has never been harmed. The devout, therefore, believe it has miraculous powers to cure and grant favors.

Thousands of people come for Sinulug. On Saturday, believers throng the Basilica, the church where the image is kept. Late in the afternoon, the Santo Niño, dressed in new clothes, is pulled through the streets on a flower-decorated *carroza.*

After a festival mass on Sunday, crowds jam the sidewalks to watch a parade. Some floats commemorate the coming of the Church and Magellan. Even more honor the early Cebuanos, particularly Lapulapu, who defeated him. Most of all, they honor the Santo Niño.

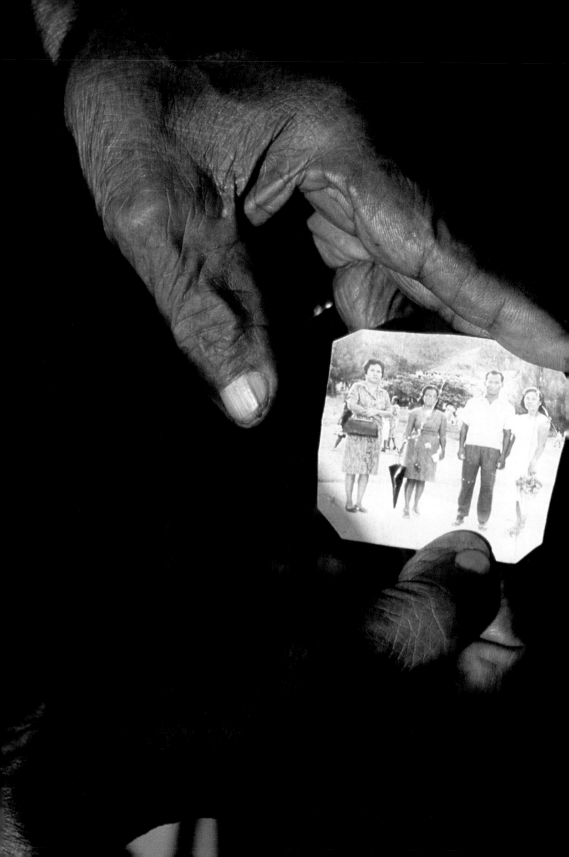

6. *Family Life:* Mabuhay *and* Masarap*!*

Mabuhay. Welcome! *Mabuhay* is the common greeting to visitors. Welcome to our country. Welcome to our home. Because the word literally means "to live," Filipinos welcome guests with the wish for long life. A visitor is immediately offered nibbles and something to drink, or if the family is eating a meal, urged to join them.

Masarap. Delicious! *Masarap* is the compliment paid to tasty cooking. Food is an important part of family gatherings and holidays: hot ginger tea and *bibingka* (rice cakes cooked over charcoal) after the dawn mass at Christmas; crisp *lechon* (whole roast pig) for the fiesta; *pastillas* (milk candy) a favorite aunt makes for birthdays.

Anyone who goes on a trip brings back local specialties to share with family and friends. Mangoes from Cebu. Strawberries from Baguio, in the Luzon mountains. *Kalamay* (coconut jam) from Bohol. *Churacha* (meaty red crabs) from Zamboanga.

Closely knit extended families, warm hospitality,

Close-knit family ties are the heart of Filipino life.

and tasty food are bound together at the heart of Philippine life.

Close Family Ties

Whether rich or poor, Philippine families have much in common. A household may consist of only parents and their children. However, family ties, and the obligation to help one another, extend to the whole clan. Everyone in town knows who is related to whom. This does not mean Filipino families are always happy and cooperative. Angry splits within families happen. They are as hard to smooth over as family fights elsewhere.

A Philippine father heads his household. He is said to be the chief breadwinner even if his wife works outside the home, as many Philippine women do. When Papa comes home, he is pampered. The children run to make him comfortable. His wife fixes his favorite food.

A Philippine mother manages the house and the money. She does the housework or sees that it is done, frequently in addition to being employed elsewhere. She also makes many of the day-to-day family decisions. In times of trouble, she holds the family together.

Historically, Philippine women have had power in the community. Mrs. Aquino was the first woman president. But women hold many other positions such as accountants, clerks, doctors, farmers, judges, senators, lawyers, mayors, and professors.

Children are brought up knowing they owe their parents—particularly their mothers—a debt of gratitude that cannot be repaid. Everyone shows respect to the elderly, whether it be grandparents or aunts and uncles. They are usually cared for at home in their old age.

Mansions and Nipa Huts

Philippine homes vary greatly. If the family is wealthy, the house may be large, modern, exquisitely furnished, and equipped with the latest gadgets. Or it may be a century old, built with coral rock and wood, and furnished with fine antiques. Instead of glass, old-style windows have tiny panes of shell scraped thin.

Most Filipinos live more simply. In town, houses are frequently made of wood. Some are made of cinder block, with tin roofs. Families also live above stores. Most dwellings have only a few rooms, which must be shared.

In the barrios, tiny houses are clustered together, without roads or sidewalks. When it rains, the paths are muddy rivers. Some barrios have electricity and running water. Others do not.

In cities, homeless families sleep on the sidewalks. Or they become squatters, building shacks of corrugated tin or even cardboard on unused land.

Rural houses are often built on stilts, with woven split-bamboo siding and nipa (palm frond) roofs. The floors are split-bamboo slats. They are springy to walk on and make comfortable beds when the sleeping mats are spread on them. The bath, toilet, and kitchen are in separate buildings. Usually, the kitchen has three stones to hold a pot over a wood fire.

Household Tasks

In wealthier homes, there is lots of help: a cook in the kitchen, maids to wash clothes and watch the children, someone to drive the car. Even in simple households, an unmarried aunt or country relation may live with the family to help with housework and child care.

Most children, particularly girls, start chores before they are six. They watch younger brothers and sisters, help wash and peel vegetables, and run errands. On farms, even small boys are sent to bring in the carabao, if the family has one. Gathering firewood is another childhood chore.

In poor households, children start helping the family earn money at an early age. Boys and girls assist at market stalls. They walk around markets hawking garlic or plastic bags. They mind their mother's *sari-sari* store (a tiny shop that sells everything from canned milk and soft drinks to notebooks and cigarettes). Boys are on the streets before daylight peddling newspapers, cigarettes, and candies. Girls string and sell jasmine flowers.

Many Filipinos, particularly women and children, spend lots of time and energy carrying water. Not every community has running water, although more and more do. A barrio family may carry bucketfuls daily for bathing, cooking, washing, and cleaning. A five-gallon bucket of water weighs about 40 pounds. Sometimes, the well or river is several miles away. No wonder washing and bathing are done in the stream if one is nearby. In urban slums, women sit in line for hours at the public faucet to get water.

To Market

Big cities have supermarkets, but many Filipinos buy their food in traditional open markets. They shop frequently because they like food fresh.

Main markets in towns are never empty. Crowds start coming about 5:30 in the morning and increase until 9:30 or so. Another crowd comes late in the afternoon. In smaller towns, the market may be open only one or two days a week.

Shoppers usually start in the wet market. It is called this because the cement floor is always slippery with water the vendors used to wash their stalls. This is the place to buy meat, mainly pork, freshly butchered, fish still flopping, and chickens recently plucked or still alive.

Women in rural areas often do the family wash in a stream.

Nearby are stalls that sell vegetables, seasonings, fruits, dried fish, and rice.

Rice and Viand

Rice is so important to Filipinos that they have many words for it. In Tagalog, for instance, *palay* is rice that is harvested but not cleaned. *Bigas* is cleaned and ready to cook. *Sinaing* is still cooking in the pot. *Kanin* is ready to eat. *Lugao* is soft rice porridge. *Puto* are steamed rice cakes. Rice can be white, brown, red, or glutenous (sweet and sticky). Each type is cooked and used differently.

If they can afford it, Filipinos eat three rice-based meals a day. But for many, a hunk of bread in the morning, a plate of rice with a bit of dry fish and vegetables later, and maybe a few bananas are the day's meals. In the Visayas, corn is almost as important as rice. When they have nothing else, Filipinos fill up on *kamoteng* (cassava), a starchy root.

Because rice is bland, Filipinos prefer their viands (main dishes) slightly sour or salty. Garlic, vinegar, soy sauce, and *patis* are favorite seasonings. *Patis* is a thin, amber-colored, salty liquid made from shrimp or fish. Filipinos add it to everything. In some parts of the country, chili pepper, ginger, and coconut milk are important ingredients. Each person also mixes a *sawsawan,* or "dipping sauce," to flavor the food to his or her own taste.

At everyday meals, Filipinos eat an enormous variety of vegetables. Green leaves, foot-long green beans, banana flowers, the heart of the coconut palm, young fern fronds, pumpkin, and eggplant are just a few. Party food, however, has few vegetables. They are too ordinary.

Filipinos enjoy many kinds of fruits. Big bananas are for cooking; middle-size and little ones are for eating. Pineapples and papayas are common. In some places, so are mangoes. The rambutan fruit has a hairy red peel and a sweet whitish flesh. Lanzones are bigger than a marble and so good it is impossible to eat just one.

The coconut is versatile. The tree trunk is tapped for its sap, *tuba,* which is drunk fresh or fermented. *Buko* is young coconut. Its water is drunk, its flesh eaten. Grated coconut flavors many dishes. Squeezed, the coconut yields *gata* (coconut milk). Coconut oil is used for cooking.

Let's Eat

Sinigang—vegetables with shrimp, fish, or meat simmered in a lightly soured broth—is perhaps the most common dish. Adobo, a stew of pork and chicken seasoned with soy sauce, vinegar, and garlic, is often called the national dish.

The Chinese brought many now-Philippine dishes. *Pancit* (noodles topped with vegetables, fish, and meat) is eaten everywhere, anytime. *Lumpia,* either fried or not, is the Philippine egg roll. Spanish dishes have also been absorbed into Philippine fare. They include heavy stews, stuffed fowl, paella (rice and seafood), and elaborate desserts. Because they are so rich, they are fiesta specialties.

Many Filipinos never seem to stop eating. In addition to breakfast, lunch, and dinner, some enjoy a snack at midmorning and have *merienda,* a substantial meal, in the late afternoon. Vendors sell snacks along the sidewalk, outside the school, by the church, wherever people pass.

This Filipino woman is off to sell her produce in an open market.

It may be bits of grilled meat, green mango, boiled peanuts, or sugarcane sticks. All of it is tasty, and best when shared with family and friends!

Tita Evelyn's *Champarado*

Believe it or not, it gets chilly in the Philippines. At least early mornings in January and February feel chilly compared to the hotter months. That is a good time to have *champarado* for breakfast. Start by making *lugao,* the soft rice porridge that Filipinos serve in many ways. Then stir in cocoa and honey. Yum. Or, as Filipinos say, *masarap.*

> 1/2 cup long grain rice (not Uncle Ben's converted rice or instant)
> 2 cups water
> 8 tbs cocoa powder (unsweetened)
> 4 tsp honey

Wash the rice. Put rice and water in a covered pan. Simmer slowly until rice is soft and mushy. Remove from the heat. Add the cocoa and honey. Mix well. Makes 4 tummy-warming servings.

7. *Education for Everyone*

At 7:30 in the morning all over the Philippines, students and teachers stand at attention in school yards, saluting as the flag is raised. They say the Philippine pledge of allegiance and sing "Bayang Magiliw," the national anthem. The principal or a senior teacher makes announcements. Then everyone files into the classrooms. And so the school day begins.

Doing well in school is important to Filipinos. Parents instill in their children the belief that education offers them an opportunity to improve their lives. Neatly framed diplomas and graduation photographs are given a place of honor in Philippine homes. Eighty-eight out of every hundred Filipinos over the age of 14 can read and write. In Japan, this figure is 99 percent; in Singapore, 87 percent; and in Indonesia and the United States, 85 percent.

School is also important for its friendships. Classmates and others who attended the same school, like family, can count on one another over the years.

Schools: Both Public and Private

The Philippine constitution requires the government to

provide ten years of free public school for all children. Elementary schools comprise Grade 1 through Grade 6. (*Grade 5* is how Filipinos usually both write and say the grade level, rather than *fifth grade*.) Following that, there are four-year high schools.

Children aged seven (Grade 1) through twelve (Grade 6) must attend school. About 95 percent of Philippine children attend elementary school and 57 percent attend high school. How many drop out before or during high school varies from community to community. In poorer areas, the dropout rate is high since youngsters need to work.

Most boys and girls attend public schools. These are secular (not religious), although optional religion classes are taught. Public schools provide books, paper, and even pencils or pens. The government does not have as much money for schools as it would like, however. Teachers' pay is low and schools are often short of books and supplies.

Students whose families can afford the costs often attend private schools. Many of these are boys' or girls' schools run by Catholic religious orders. Tuition at these schools is high. Many parents scrimp and save to pay the fees. Even so, most children who go to private schools are from well-off families.

The best private schools offer more years of schooling than the public schools. They start with one or two years

Waiting for school to start

of preschool for five- and six-year-olds. Some extend elementary school to Grade 7. Beyond high school, the best may also have colleges.

All the schools in the country, public and private, are under the supervision of the Department of Education and Culture in Manila. The department decides what subjects will be taught, what books will be used, and when classes will be in session, even for the private schools.

The school year starts in June and ends in March. April and May are extremely hot and not a comfortable time to be studying. There is a holiday over Christmas and New Year.

In most schools, the day begins with the 7:30 A.M. flag raising. Classes start at 8:00 and continue until noon, with one short recess. There is an hour's break for lunch. Then school resumes until 5:00 in the evening. Each class may have 40 to 50 students. Some city public schools are so crowded that they run two sessions.

Some high schools are academic, preparing their students for university. Others are vocational, offering a wide range of technical training. High school graduates must pass the National College Entrance Examination (NCEE) to go further. Higher education ranges from one- or two-year technical courses to four-year colleges to universities offering master's and doctor's degrees. The University of the Philippines, which has several campuses, is run by the government. Most colleges and technical schools are privately owned and operated.

Mababang Paaralan

Public elementary schools are easy to recognize. Across the front is a big sign: MABABANG PAARALAN NG ____ and the town name (elementary school of ____). School buildings in smaller communities are often one long, single story raised off the ground on stilts. A wide porch frequently runs the length of the school.

Most schools are a cluster of buildings. The classrooms are usually arranged so the front and back walls have big windows that allow breezes in. Covered walkways often connect the buildings so that during the rainy season people can stay dry.

Rest rooms are in a separate building. Schools usually do not have drinking fountains, and students often bring their own drinking water from home in small plastic bottles. Some schools have shops that sell snacks. If students live close enough, they go home for lunch. Otherwise, they bring their food or the money to buy it.

Private schools usually have more impressive buildings and grounds than public schools. They also have better libraries, audiovisual equipment, computers, laboratories, and more extracurricular activities.

Private-school students wear simple uniforms. Some

public-school students wear uniforms as well. Interestingly, teachers also wear uniforms. Filipinos believe this fosters school unity and identity. It also makes teachers easy to spot and reinforces their authority.

What Subjects?

Classes are taught in English except for Grade 1. For that year only, teachers use the local language children speak at home. That way children start the basics of reading and numbers without having to learn them in a new language. English and Pilipino are introduced as subjects. By the next year, students are expected to be able to understand English fairly well.

The work load is intense. The main subjects are usually taught in the morning and the early afternoon. Later in the afternoon is the time for physical education, music, and vocational classes. Even the youngest students are assigned homework almost every night.

Philippine students study many subjects: math, science, Philippine history, government, social science, civics, Pilipino, and English. In Grade 6, students read excerpts from José Rizal, the Philippines' most famous writer, and *Beowulf,* the old English epic. They diagram sentences and study algebra and general science.

At all levels, children learn about the various Philippine tribal cultures. However, they are taught that

The school day begins with morning flag-raising.

the Philippines, though varied, is one country. The idea that "we are all Filipinos" is stressed.

Civics teaches behavior that is considered necessary for community life. This includes proper manners and social values taught in practical terms. Typical lessons are: Find your parents and greet them when you get home. Keep the school grounds clean.

Both boys and girls study home economics, which includes simple cooking, sewing, ideas about family life, and sex education. Even in city schools, vegetable gardening is taught with an emphasis on good nutrition as well as basic agriculture. The students have garden plots on the school grounds.

Physical education is always popular. Boys and girls play volleyball, tug-of-war, baseball, and sometimes basketball. For the school Sports Day, students and teachers divide into teams, which compete in track and field events.

Rules and Awards

Philippine schools are strict and formal. School rules are clearly stated and expected to be obeyed absolutely. In the classroom the teacher holds a position of respect and authority.

In this sense, Filipinos are still strongly influenced by Spanish teaching methods as well as their own traditions. Younger Filipinos defer to their elders. Anything else is rude and shameful. Teachers take the place of parents in the schoolroom. Students are expected to show them the same respect they would give their parents.

Students are expected to work diligently. Excelling is encouraged and rewarded. Exams are given in every subject every six weeks. The results are tabulated, students are ranked, and class standings are announced. At the end of the year students take exams covering everything they have studied.

The closing awards and graduation ceremony highlights the school year. Everyone comes: parents, aunts, uncles, grandparents, brothers, sisters. The mayor, municipal council, and other dignitaries sit with the principal on a stage that has been erected for the occasion.

The top students in each class, starting with Grade 1, are awarded medals for valedictorian, salutatorian, and first, second, and third honors. A tie for any of these honors is often broken by a runoff exam several days before the ceremony. Each winner and his or her parents come forward to receive the medal from the mayor. Proud relatives shower the winner with orchid leis. Flashbulbs pop.

Sometimes a relative puts an advertisement in the local paper with the awardee's picture, congratulating both the student and the parents. Congratulatory ads are even more common for high school and college graduates who excel. Institutions whose students take national qualifying examinations—medical, law, or accounting schools, for instance—place ads honoring their top finishers. Such honors are not just for the individual students. They bring credit and status to families and institutions.

From the Spanish and Americans

Western education in the Philippines has a long history. When the Spaniards first arrived, they established an educational system controlled by the priests. Santo Tomas, the oldest university still operating in the Philippines, was founded in 1611. (Harvard, the oldest university in the United States, opened in 1636.) Colleges for both men and women were opened in Manila and Cebu in the late 16th century. Originally, these schools were open only to the children of Spaniards. In 1863 the Spanish government made education available to the *indios.*

The present system of free public schools is perhaps the greatest contribution that the Americans made to the Philippines. Among their first decisions was to establish primary schools. These classes were taught in English. This gave the country, for the first time, a language to link all the people. English also linked Filipinos to the English-speaking world beyond their shores.

Perhaps most importantly, the Americans gave the children of ordinary people, not just the children of the rich, the opportunity to go to school.

Even so, these were not Filipino schools. Young Filipinos were taught American songs, American history, American values. Philippine ideals, culture, and patriots were not taught until after the formation of the Commonwealth in 1935.

Nonetheless, the seeds of public education were planted in fertile soil. A population that can read and write with a thirst for education is one of the Philippines' major advantages as it struggles toward a better future.

8. Spiderfights, Beetle Jousts, and Basketball

Do you know where the yo-yo came from? That's right. When the yo-yo was patented in the United States in the 1930s, the Philippines was listed as its origin. Soon yo-yos became popular all over the world. But children in the Philippines have played with them so long no one knows whether they were invented there or came from elsewhere.

Filipino boys and girls play many of the same games children the world over play. Some of their pastimes are common throughout Southeast Asia. Others are special to a small part of the Philippines.

Young Filipinos often make their own playthings. This is not surprising. Children everywhere love to play and are inventive. Most Filipino children have little extra money for toys. But the world around them is full of possibilities.

Filipinos young and old enjoy sports. Anybody reading the sports pages of Philippine newspapers will find stories about basketball, soccer (which they call football), tennis, boxing, even golf. There is also coverage of international sports: the Super Bowl, the

World Series, and the Olympics. On the same page, there might be a story about cockfighting.

Cockfighting

Cockfighting has been a Filipino passion for centuries. The roar of spectators at the cockpit is as familiar a sound as the crowing of cocks before dawn.

Cockpits are square buildings with a ring, or pit, in the center. Steep bleachers surround the pit on all sides. On fight day, the cockpit is often so crowded that boys cling to the rafters or perch on open window ledges.

A full fight card lasts all afternoon or evening. Two handlers release their birds in the pit. Each cock has been "heeled" with tiny sharpened blades. Naturally combative, the roosters attack each other, pecking and slashing. Each fight is over in seconds. The winner survives to fight another day; the loser is carried home to the cooking pot.

Fighting cocks are specially bred, cared for, and trained. A good one is prized by its owner and can cost thousands of pesos. (In 1992, 28 pesos, the Philippine currency, equaled one U.S. dollar.) Sometimes owners train their birds themselves, or they hire famous handlers to do so. Whoever is handling them spends hours each day fondling his birds. There are many outstanding local breeds. However, the fiercest, the Texas, was introduced after World War I. Its name tells where it came from.

Betting is what cockfighting is all about. Thousands, even millions, of pesos can ride on a single fight. A complicated betting system has evolved over time. Bets are placed with a nod of the head or wave of a finger. The person holding the bets keeps track of it all in his head. Bets are settled after the fight is over.

Spiderfights and Beetle Jousts

If grown-ups have cockfights, Filipino boys have spiderfights and beetle jousts. These are among the many ways children create fun with what is around them.

The best time to catch spiders is early morning when the dew glistening on their webs makes them easier to see. Many boys believe that the slim black spiders that live in tamarind or guava trees are the best. A spider that fights back when it is cornered is the fiercest. Boys keep their spiders in little matchboxes that tuck easily into their pockets. Several can be put in one box if it has cardboard dividers to keep them apart. Spiders eat flies. They will live a long time inside a matchbox if their owners catch some flies and feed them every day.

Two boys pit their fighters against each other. The spiders are put on a stick held out straight. They go at each other with their fangs. The fight is usually to the death. Boys may well bet a centavo or two on the outcome if they have the money. (One peso is worth 100 centavos.)

Fighting cocks are prized by their owners.

Beetle jousts are held in the summertime when fat black rhinoceros beetles fall out of the trees. These beetles are prized for their strong backs. They make good pets that will curl up and sleep in your hand if they are gently patted.

There are many games to play with beetles. Two beetles are put one on top of the other, back to back. The top beetle tries to balance itself while the bottom one tries to run away. If the top one stays put, it and its owner win. Beetles are also raced, but not for speed and distance. Each boy puts his beetle down on its back. The first one to turn itself over wins.

It is often difficult for people outside the Philippines to understand how important cock or insect fights are to many Filipinos. Outsiders find it hard to accept competitions involving animals. However, these activities have been part of Philippine culture for centuries.

Make Your Own

Filipino children make many kinds of playthings themselves. They usually make their own kites. January to March, when the skies are blue and the winds blow, is kite season. Little boys fly a *boca-boca,* a small square piece of paper on a short string. Older boys try the *chapi-chapi,* the familiar diamond-shaped kite flown all over the world. Grown men fly the *gurion,* a huge kite with a strong bamboo frame. These can be fighting kites if the string is dipped in glue and ground glass. Opponents try to cut one another's strings as they fly the kites high in the air. A strip of leaf fastened on the frame makes a kite buzz like a bumblebee.

A boy's *tirador,* or slingshot, is often his prized possession. He tucks it in to his back pocket or in his belt and carries it with him everywhere. He often uses it to knock down ripe fruit on the trees in the neighborhood. A regular family chore for many boys is to use their sling-shots to keep the birds out of the fields.

Homemade slingshots are the best. Guava trees, with their forked branches, provide the ideal wood for making slingshots. Clever boys tie up a fork while it is still in the tree so that it grows equally balanced. When the branch is about as thick as a thumb, it is cut from the tree. It is then heated over a flame so that the sides of the fork can be pulled slightly closer together. Afterward, the bark is removed and the wood is smoothed to a nice sheen. The sling is often a rubber strip cut out of an old inner tube.

Few Filipino boys make their own wooden tops anymore, although some people in the southern Philippines still do. Homemade or store-bought, tops are a favorite toy and top-spinning contests are a popular pastime. The simplest game is to see which top spins the longest. By spinning them cleverly, boys get their tops to hit others out of a circle or even split an opponent's top in two.

Jumping, Tag, and Make-Believe Bullfights

Filipino boys and girls delight in many games that are familiar to children all over the world. They have jumping contests they call *luksong tinik,* which means "jumping the spine." Sometimes one person jumps over a stick that is raised higher and higher by others holding it. Sometimes several children create a barrier by stacking first their feet and then their hands one on top of the other.

Or they play *tanguan,* hide-and-seek. They choose all sorts of hiding places—even the tops of trees. Filipino girls like to play *piko,* or hopscotch.

Then there is *patintero,* a kind of team tag that is often played on warm, moonlit nights when no one wants to stay inside. Players draw a court on the ground. They make three long parallel lines and crosscut them with three other lines. Instead of just scratching the lines in the dirt, they use a watering can to trace the lines twice with a slow, wet drizzle. That way, the lines stay visible for a long time. The point is to run from one side of the court to the other and back again without getting tagged by the other team. The intersecting lines make bases that are safe.

Many contests are part of fiestas. *Palo sebo,* or "greased pole," is a favorite. A tall, strong bamboo pole slickly greased with coconut oil is set up in the town plaza. At the top is a prize, maybe a bag of money or a small bag of candy. Whoever climbs to the top first wins it.

In *juego de anillo* a rider spears a ring hanging from a bamboo arch. Years ago the best horsemen played. Today the riders are on bicycles.

Juego de toro is a make-believe bullfight. The bull is made of papier-mâché and decorated with long strings of firecrackers. A man climbs inside. After the fireworks are lit, the bull charges here and there, sizzling and popping.

The prize goes to whoever catches the bull before the explosions stop.

Sipa

Girls and boys both play *sipa:* kicking a shuttlecock to keep it up in the air. Kicks can be executed with the inside, outside, or top of the foot, the heel, the toe, the knee, the shoulder, even the top of the head. But the shuttle may not be touched with the hands after the starting toss.

Small children see how long they can keep a light shuttle up. Each kick scores one. In one turn, a good player can keep the shuttle up over a hundred kicks. The secret is to maintain a steady rhythm. As children get older, they play in teams, either passing the shuttle around a circle from player to player or back and forth over a net like a volleyball.

Shuttlecocks can be bought in stores, but homemade ones are best. A flat lead washer provides the weight. The flier is made of bright strips of cellophane or tissue paper pulled through the hole of the washer and fastened. The ends are left loose and fluffy. The bushier the flier, the more stable the shuttle. Little children often make shuttles out of waxed paper folded into cubes. They blow into the cubes from time to time. This keeps the cubes full of air so they bounce nicely with each kick.

In the countryside children make their shuttles by

weaving strips of buri palm or coconut leaf into a hollow cube. These fly beautifully. Grown-ups play with a round ball made of split rattan.

Sipa is played all over Southeast Asia and *sipa* competitions are held throughout the region.

Hoop-crazed

Basketball-crazy is a good description of the Philippines. The game is played everywhere. Because most Filipinos are short and agile, their playing style emphasizes speed and shooting skill.

Even the smallest barangay has a patch of hard-packed dirt and a basketball hoop outside the community hall. Walk three hours away from the road up the mountains of Mindoro to a Mangyan settlement and there will be a basketball court. After a day in the fields, the whole village gathers to watch the young men play before it gets dark. In city squatter areas men and boys clear places to play. They even attach lights illegally to electric lines so they can play at night.

Politicians campaigning for election keep basketballs in the backs of their vehicles to hand out to their supporters. Someone who wants to be mayor will build courts in different parts of town, assuming the voters will remember when election time comes.

Most municipalities have leagues. Businesses usually

Basketball hoops sprout up all over the Philippines, even along the beaches.

sponsor the teams. In bigger towns the teams are semipro or professional. The best pro teams are in Manila, but people all over the country root for them. The teams are named after their company sponsors: Alaska Milk (known as the Milkmen), Genebra San Miguel, A & W Hamburger. Like the game itself, some players are imported from the United States. But many of the good ones are Filipino.

Whether their games have come from across the seas or have originated in the islands, Filipino children love to play them.

9. Coming to America

The first Filipinos to settle in North America came before the American Revolution. Most, however, arrived after 1898, when the Philippines became a U.S. colony. Today there are nearly 1.5 million Filipino Americans. They make up the fastest-growing and second-largest Asian community in the United States. Only the Chinese exceed them in numbers.

Like Philippine history, the story of Filipinos in America is marked by many hardships and struggles. It is also a record of hard work, proud achievements, and important contributions to American life.

Manilamen: First Filipino Immigrants

The first Filipinos to settle in North America were known as Manilamen. They had been forced by the Spanish in the 1600s to work on the galleons and had jumped ship in the New World. They settled around Acapulco, Mexico, and Baja California. By 1763 some were living on the coast of what is now Louisiana. Fertile fishing grounds made it easy for them to earn a living. Their simple life was similar to the way they had lived back home on the islands. In their new village of St. Malo, they had little reason to learn more than a few English words for trading. As time passed, later arrivals formed other villages and married local women. Some of these families are now in their tenth generation in Louisiana.

Some seamen settled in New Orleans, a port where they got work on ships sailing the Atlantic Ocean. As city dwellers, they quickly became part of local life. By the middle of the 19th century, some had opened small shops and businesses. Today the descendants of the Manilamen are an integral part of the community in New Orleans.

Students Step Ashore

Unlike the Manilamen, most Filipino immigrants came to the United States after 1898. The first of these was a small group of students seeking training in American colleges and universities.

Most of these young men and women were from well-to-do families. They became doctors, lawyers, nurses, teachers, and engineers. Many returned home and became leaders.

Others stayed in America. Some married Filipinos they met in the United States. Some sent for a husband or wife who had been left behind. Still others married

Americans. Many of these families are now prominent in Filipino communities in West Coast cities.

Cane Workers Arrive in Hawaii

Between 1905 and 1920 thousands of Filipino laborers were recruited to work in Hawaiian sugarcane fields. Chinese and Japanese agricultural workers had been brought in earlier. Unlike them, Filipinos entered the country freely and could not be forced to leave easily. They were protected because they came from an American colony. But they did not have full rights as citizens.

These workers, or *sakadas,* as they called themselves, were lured by visions of easy money and a better life. Their dreams were to return home triumphantly sporting handfuls of dollars and fancy American clothes.

The *sakadas* signed contracts agreeing to work for three years. They received transportation to Hawaii, wages of about $18 a month, housing, and medical care. Men usually came alone. Although a few women and children came, the sugarcane companies discouraged families.

Life was difficult for the *sakadas.* Their work was backbreaking. Their housing was usually only a barracks with a washhouse outside. Although there were other Asian workers, their housing was segregated, or separated, by race. There were separate "villages" for the white managers, Spanish or Portuguese overseers, and each group of the Asian laborers. Most *sakadas* were extremely lonely because their families were not with them. Labor disputes and strikes were frequent and often violent.

Nonetheless, these Filipinos managed to send back much of their hard-earned money to the Philippines. But despite their earlier dreams only one in three of them returned home to live.

With the Great Depression in the 1930s the world sugar industry collapsed. Filipinos left the cane fields for better wages in the pineapple and coffee plantations, which were not quite so badly affected. Some also managed to leave the hard labor of the fields for jobs in hospitals, hotels, and canneries. Others gradually became dockworkers or got jobs on the U.S. military bases in Hawaii. Some started their own small shops and restaurants.

A Great Wave of Immigrants

In the 1920s a great flow of Filipino men, or *pinoys,* as the immigrants called themselves, came to the American mainland. At this time there were no rules, or quotas, restricting the number of Filipinos who could enter the United States. The *pinoys* came seeking work. Many settled in California, where there is still a very large Filipino-American community.

The *pinoys,* like other unskilled immigrants, were limited in the jobs they could get. In the cities, they often worked in restaurants. In the countryside, they harvested vegetables. Employers ignorantly believed that Filipinos, being shorter, could stoop more easily than American workers.

By the 1930s some 25,000 *pinoys* were working in the San Joaquin Valley of California. These farm laborers moved from place to place. They stayed in an area only as long as a particular crop needed planting or harvesting. When there was no farm work to be had, they went to the Alaskan fish canneries. Hardier Filipinos stayed on in Alaska to process crab and shrimp. Filipino workers have been a major source of labor for the canneries for the past 60 years.

Because there were few Filipino women in California—one for every 14 Filipino men—life was difficult for the *pinoys.* Americans did not want them to socialize with American women. People also resented the jobs the *pinoys* took. Many restaurants and dance halls posted signs saying FILIPINOS NOT ALLOWED. Laws were passed in California, as well as in 14 other states, that made it illegal for white people to marry people of other races, destroying many mixed marriages and preventing many more. The California law was repealed in 1948.

Pinays

Pinay is the word used for Filipino women who immigrated to the United States. Before World War II, the *pinays* generally had been better educated back home than the *pinoys* they married in the United States.

These women worked with their husbands in the fields or cooked for the work crews. Some opened small businesses. *Pinays* became professionals sooner than the immigrant men did. In California the first Filipino-American teachers were women. In New York, they were nurses. The first Filipino pharmacist in Washington State was a woman. *Pinays* often found work in offices and other places where Filipino men were not welcome.

Pinays held their families together in the face of many difficulties. They made sure that their children attended school. They kept the Filipino traditions alive. Their importance to the Filipino-American communities far outweighed their numbers.

Stopping the Flow

In 1935, when the Philippines became a commonwealth, the steady flow of Filipino immigration came to a halt. Filipinos lost their special status as a colony and became subject to the same quota limitations as other Asians. Only 50 Filipinos were allowed to immigrate a year. The

Filipino Americans, like this dietician at a hospital in California, make many important contributions to American life.

annual quota for Asians was considerably smaller than for Europeans.

Another law passed in 1935 provided money to pay the fares of any Filipinos who would return home voluntarily. Few people took advantage of this. Filipinos in both the United States and the Philippines were insulted by this law. *Pinoys* also felt that if they accepted government money, their relatives would know they had not become rich. They would feel ashamed.

During the U.S. involvement in World War II, from 1941 to 1945, immigration was suspended. After the war, Filipinos who served in the U.S. armed forces were given special rights to immigrate. In 1946 the Filipino quota was increased to 100 people a year.

The New Wave

The small quota remained until 1965. That year the United States finally revised its immigration laws. The new law gave each country, including the Philippines, an annual quota of 20,000 people. Many more Filipinos still want to immigrate to the United States than are allowed by the law.

The change set off a wave of Filipino migration that still continues. Many are doctors, surgeons, dentists, nurses, pharmacists, and nutritionists. These newcomers often have found work before they come.

Whether they are newcomers or have been in the United States for several generations, Filipino Americans maintain their strong family ties. They also belong to numerous social organizations, and they continue to support their countrymen "back home." When the islands are struck by disasters like earthquakes or volcanic eruptions, Filipino Americans rush to send aid.

Like many immigrant minority groups, Filipino Americans often struggle to maintain their traditions in a culture very different from their own. They try, for example, to teach their children the age-old custom of respect for elders.

A Contributing Community

The largest Filipino-American communities are still in California, particularly around Los Angeles and San Francisco. Chicago, Seattle, Dallas, Washington D.C., and New York also have sizable communities. Each city has Filipino newspapers, stores, restaurants, and places of entertainment.

Filipino Americans have made many contributions to the United States. They have served with distinction in the U.S. military, particularly the navy, since World War I. Filipino labor was important in making Hawaii prosperous. Because of their difficult working conditions, *pinoys* became active labor leaders, first within their own

Many Filipino Americans own shops in their local communities.

community and later in the national labor movement. Pablo Manlapit founded the Filipino Federation of Labor, Hawaii's first Filipino union, in 1911.

Flyweights Pancho Villa, Dado Marino, and Flash Elorde were world champion boxers. Vicki Manalo Draves became the first woman in Olympic history to win both the high and low diving gold medals in 1948.

Filipino Americans are at the forefront of American medicine. Many are nurses and doctors around the country. Dr. Jorge Garcia of Washington D.C. is a leading heart surgeon.

Filipino-American women also play key national roles. Irene Natividad led the National Women's Political Caucus in the 1980s, helping to expand opportunities for all women. Josie Cruz Natori heads one of the top lingerie businesses in the country. Lilia Clemente is a noted financier.

Whenever and however they came to the United States, Filipinos brought determination, endurance, and a capacity for hard work. As they settled, they, their children, and their children's children added their strengths to the rich fabric of American life.

Appendix

Philippine Embassies and Consulates in the United States and Canada

Philippine embassies and consulates offer help to Americans and Canadians who want to know more about the Philippines. Write or call the one nearest you:

In the United States

Embassy of the Philippines
1617 Massachusetts Avenue, N.W.
Washington, D.C. 20036
(202) 483-1414

Philippine Consulate General
Suite 2100
30 North Michigan Avenue
Chicago, Illinois 60602
(312) 332-6458/59

Philippine Consulate General
Texas Commerce Bank Building
5177 Richmond Avenue
Houston, Texas 77056
(713) 621-8618

Philippine Consulate General
2433 Pali Highway
Honolulu, Hawaii 96817
(808) 595-6316

Philippine Consulate General
Philippine Center Building
556 Fifth Avenue
New York, New York 10036
(212) 764-1330

Philippine Consulate General
Suite 900
3660 Wilshire Boulevard
Los Angeles, California 90010
(313) 387-5321

Philippine Consulate General
Philippine Center Building, 6th Floor
447 Sutter Street
San Francisco, California 94108
(415) 433-6666

Philippine Consulate General
Suite 801
United Airlines Building
2033 Sixth Avenue
Seattle, Washington 98121
(206) 441-1640

In Canada

Embassy of the Philippines
130 Albert Street
Ottawa, Ontario KIP 5G4
Canada
(613) 233-1121

Consulate
151 Bloor Street, Room 365
Toronto, Ontario M58-184
Canada
(416) 922-7181

Consulate General
470 Grandville Street, Suite 301-8
Vancouver, B.C. V6C-1V5
Canada
(604) 685-7645

Selected Bibliography

Agoncillo, Teodoro A. and Milagros C. Guerro. *History of the Filipino People.* Quezon City, Philippines: R.P. Garcia Publishing Company, 1986.

Bellwood, Peter. *Man's Conquest of the Pacific, the Prehistory of Southeast Asia and Oceania.* New York: Oxford University Press, 1979.

Insight Guide to the Philippines. New York: Prentice-Hall, 1989.

Karnow, Stanley. *In Our Image: America's Empire in the Philippines.* New York: Random House, 1989.

Pido, Antonio J.A. *The Pilipinos in America.* New York: Center for Migration Studies, 1986.

Steinberg, David Joel. *The Philippines, A Singular and a Plural Place.* 2d ed. Boulder: Westview Press, 1990.

_____. *In Search of Southeast Asia, A Modern History.* Rev. ed. Honolulu: University of Hawaii Press, 1987.

United States Department of State. *Philippines Background Notes.* August 1986.

Index

About the Author and Photographer

Margaret Sullivan first arrived in the Philippines in 1971. She lived in Cebu City until 1974 with her husband and four children. Since then, she has returned to the country regularly. Born in China, she has spent half her life in Asia. She is a writer and intercultural communications specialist whose articles have appeared in numerous magazines and newspapers. This is her first children's book. Ms. Sullivan is now based in McLean, Virginia, but goes "home" to Asia whenever she can.

Mark Downey is a photographer and professor of photojournalism at California State University, Hayward. He has made four trips to the Philippines, one especially for this book. He covers world cultures for national and international magazines. His work has appeared in such publications as *National Geographic, Geo, U.S. News & World Report,* and *Time* magazine. Based in Alameda, California, Mr. Downey travels frequently to Asia and has developed a special affinity for the Philippines—because of the "warmth and spirit" of the people.